UNDERSEA TERROR

ALSO BY ERNEST A. McKAY

Carrier Strike Force
Pacific Air Combat in World War II

~~~~~~~~~~~~~~~~~~~~~~~~~~~~~~~~~~~~~~~

UNDERSEA TERROR

U-BOAT WOLF PACKS IN WORLD WAR II

BY
ERNEST A. McKAY

Illustrated

JULIAN MESSNER
NEW YORK

Published by Julian Messner, a Simon & Schuster
Division of Gulf & Western Corporation.
Simon & Schuster Building,
1230 Avenue of the Americas,
New York, New York 10020.
JULIAN MESSNER and colophon are trademarks of
Simon & Schuster, registered in the U.S. Patent
and Trademark Office.
Frontispiece: Bundesarchiv Militarchiv

Manufactured in the United States of America

Design by Irving Perkins Associates

Library of Congress Cataloging in Publication Data

McKay, Ernest A.
Undersea terror.

Bibliography: p.
Includes index.
Summary: Details the activities of the German
U-boats which caused tremendous damage and loss of
life to the Allied forces during World War II.
1. World War, 1939–1945—Naval operations—
Submarine—Juvenile literature. 2. World War,
1939–1945—Naval operations, German—Juvenile
literature. [1. World War, 1939–1945—Naval
operations—Submarine. 2. World War, 1939–1945—
Naval operations, German] I. Title.
D781.M34 1982   940.54′51   82-12529

ISBN 0-671-44196-5

Acknowledgments

Special thanks are due E. Hine of the Imperial War Museum, London; Dr. Trumpp of Bundesarchiv, Koblenz, West Germany; and Robert A. Carlisle of the U.S. Navy Office of Information. My wife, Ellen, as always, was a big help with research and advice.

CONTENTS

UNDERSEA TERROR

1

SCAPA FLOW

Kapitänleutnant Günther Prien, commander of U-47, was a daring and skillful man. He was also a vain man who was undoubtedly pleased to receive an unusual call to attend a meeting with Karl Doenitz, commodore of submarines.

It was a Sunday morning, and World War II had barely begun. Doenitz had many things on his mind, yet he greeted the young officer in a friendly manner and carried on an idle conversation for a few minutes. As they talked, Prien noticed that he faced a chart of Scapa Flow, a main base for the British Royal Navy. The name itself was a deep scar on the memory of every German because the defeated Imperial Fleet of Germany had been scuttled there in humiliation after World War I.

Did Doenitz have some wild scheme to attack this seemingly impregnable fortress? Certainly it was not a new idea. Two submarines had been lost in pursuit of just this harebrained notion during World War I.

Finally, Doenitz got down to business. A surprise attack on Scapa Flow was exactly what he had in mind. For days, months, and maybe years, he had toyed with the thought. It was the dream of every German submariner. But was it merely a dream? Not long ago, while Doenitz pondered over a chart of the harbor, his clear-thinking operations officer had said, "You know, sir, I'm pretty sure we could find a way to get in." The words gave Doenitz the encouragement he needed. In the next few days he gathered all available intelligence plus a new series of detailed aerial photographs and pored over them.

Now Doenitz asked Prien if he thought it was possible to attack Scapa Flow, but he quickly added that he did not

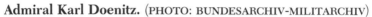
Admiral Karl Doenitz. (PHOTO: BUNDESARCHIV-MILITARCHIV)

want an immediate answer. Instead, he gave Prien a complete file on the subject. He wanted him to study it carefully in the utmost secrecy for at least forty-eight hours before giving him a reply. This was a time for careful judgment, not a fast reflex response. Doenitz impressed on Prien that he was absolutely free to turn down the assignment without any reflection on his career or character. After all, perhaps it was only a foolhardy adventure.

Nevertheless, Doenitz had carefully selected his man. He believed that, if anyone could perform this impossible mission, Prien could. A former merchant marine officer dedicated to the submarine service, Prien was full of gusto and the joy of life. It seemed always so ironic that men who enjoyed life the most were ready to risk their lives in daredevil pursuits. Prien, however, was also an extremely able seaman and a stern disciplinarian who demanded the utmost in performance from his crew. Purely and simply, he was a martinet. If he had not been so serious, it would have been laughable to see the long list of crew members whom he placed on report for the slightest infraction during a cruise. Still, his crew respected him. They knew that he was a true professional and that they were sailing with one of the best U-boat commanders in Germany.

Prien followed his orders and studied the intelligence material in minute detail. Scapa Flow was set in the midst of the Orkney Islands, north of the Scottish Highlands. The large body of water was well protected and made an excellent anchorage for the British. Strategically, the British Admiralty regarded it as the guardian of the North Sea. There was more than one entrance to the base, but man-made defenses seemed to be everywhere and one possibility after another appeared hopeless after further study. Mines, nets, and sunken ships blocked the passages, and yet strangely they were not the biggest problem.

The greatest menace for the invader was the naturally

swift current that made navigating into the Flow extremely dangerous. No U-boat had ever entered the harbor. The World War I submarines had been lost while still in the outer approaches. The difficulty was that the current moved at a speed of ten miles an hour while a submarine had an underwater speed of about seven knots. That meant that any assault would have to be attempted on the surface.

The aerial photos gave the Germans a ray of hope. A boat might slip by the sunken ships and enter through the narrow Kirk Sound. At best it was a risky business. The channel was only about fifteen meters wide, and the depth was scarcely three and a half fathoms. Nevertheless, with luck a boat might slip through during slack water between tides when there was little or no current.

Two days later Prien had his answer. He appeared at Doenitz's quarters and told him that he was ready to go ahead. His life and the lives of his crew depended on his voluntary judgment. With the decision made, the two men selected Friday, October 13, for the operation. For men looking for luck, the date was not exactly a good omen. But superstitions had little to do with the selection. That night there would be a new moon and slack water would occur during the dark hours. Sneaking through under the cover of darkness was a necessity.

Immediately the plan went into operation, but secrecy was still the byword. Doenitz informed the commander in chief, Grossadmiral Erich Raeder orally. Now, as plans went ahead, the crew sensed that something odd was afoot. Instead of taking stores on for their next cruise, they unloaded food and fuel. At least, they guessed, it would be a short cruise, but where were they headed?

After the U-47 got under way, the crew was even more surprised. Sailing through the North Sea, the aggressive captain passed up an easy target. That was unlike Prien. Curiosity overcame the capable first watch officer, Engel-

Captain Günther Prien. (PHOTO: BUNDESARCHIV)

bert Endrass. Fishing for information, he asked Prien if they were headed for the Orkneys. Prien answered, "Yes," and then added, "Hold onto something Endrass. . . . We're going into Scapa Flow."

With batteries charged and the boat submerged, Prien gathered the men into the crew's quarters and gave them the news. It electrified them, and they went back to work with new enthusiasm. The odds against them seemed to be of no consequence.

The boat approached the Orkneys underwater and then settled on the seabed until the next day. Silence was now the key word. There was every reason to believe that the British had some secret detection equipment, and the Germans did not want to give themselves away. Water is a good conductor of sound, so they took every precaution. Seamen who had to walk about the boat wrapped their shoes in rags to muffle the noise. All who were not on duty rested in their bunks until the afternoon of the thirteenth. Then they were roused and had a warm meal. No one knew when, if ever, they would eat again. After supper, the men checked their equipment once more. No one wanted to be a weak link.

At about 2000, Prien brought the boat up to periscope depth to have a look around. He saw nothing and surfaced. The weather was perfect, but now they ran into their first difficulty. Instead of a dark night the sea shone clearly, not from the moon, but from the bright northern lights, the Aurora Borealis. Prien's log noted, "It is disgustingly light. The whole bay is lit up." The night was so bright that Prien wondered whether or not he should continue. It might be wiser, he told himself, to postpone the operation until a darker night. Then he thought of the awful letdown that would be for the crew and, whether he admitted it or not, for himself. He decided that it would be better to proceed while everyone was keyed up and morale was high. On he went.

Close to Kirk Sound another threatening problem arose. The chief engineer noticed a large amount of salt water in one of the diesel engines. He reported the trouble to Prien who did not appear to appreciate the technical dangers. Or, more likely, he was too intent on his mission. He simply told the engineer that they would take care of the situation when they returned to base. The reply did not solve the trouble, but it did send the chief engineer back to the engine room realizing that he would have to find an answer himself. Cleverly, he rigged a gutter to drain the water and solve the problem temporarily.

There was no turning back now. Prien had memorized the hazards of the narrow channel, and he sailed carefully forward without taking time to refer to charts. His study paid off, and he showed his superb seamanship in the channel, which was difficult to negotiate in daylight, let alone at night. Even so, the boat went aground in the shallow waters and for a few seconds they held their breath until it freed itself. Delicately working past the sunken ships, Prien thought the ghostly blockships looked like the wings of a theater. The U-47 scraped against one, but no harm was done, and at last the boat was inside the anchorage.

Once inside the anchorage Prien was disappointed rather than elated. Where were the targets? He did not see any. The day before German aircraft had sighted an aircraft carrier, five heavy ships, and ten cruisers. Most of the British fleet had actually departed that same day. It was unbelievable. He proceeded north and sharp-eyed lookouts spotted two large shadows. All was not lost. One was a battleship, the mighty *Royal Oak,* and another behind it was erroneously identified at the time as the *Repulse.* In reality, the second ship was an obsolete aircraft carrier.

As quickly as possible, Prien closed his range and fired a salvo of torpedos at the two ships. The result was zero. Only one torpedo exploded, and that merely hit an anchor chain. The noise should have alerted the British, but surprisingly they did not respond. It sounded to them like an internal explosion. Then Prien missed with a stern shot. Once again, all was quiet.

Amazingly, the U-boat, still on the surface, remained undetected. The determined Prien decided to try again. In the middle of the main anchorage he reloaded torpedoes, a tough, sweaty job that seemed to take an eternity. Prien circled the anchorage while the men worked. Ready again, he moved closer to his target and fired from the bow. The seconds slipped into one minute, two minutes, three minutes, and then a tremendous explosion roared through the still waters. The whole salvo had found its mark and the gigantic *Royal Oak* was blown to pieces. In that disastrous instant almost 800 British seaman lost their lives.

Immediately the quiet Scapa Flow turned into a scene of pandemonium. Destroyers pulled anchor, searchlights scanned the bay, signals flashed back and forth, and men rushed helter-skelter in every direction. U-47 was now the hunted, and Prien's only objective was to make a fast getaway. How could he weave his way through this mad scene? Destroyers showed up from the southeast, and one seemed to block the way out.

Prien needed speed. He ordered, "Full ahead," and used both the diesel and the electric engines to make a hasty exit. The engines caused a noticeable wake, but Prien sneaked close to the mainland, hoping that the boat would be unseen against a background of dark hills. As he moved forward, the driver of a truck or car on the coast road directed the vehicle's headlights squarely at the submarine. Then he flashed his lights on and off as though signaling. What the driver thought, no one knows, but he turned around and rushed off from where he had come.

Next, Prien saw a destroyer speeding toward them. Perhaps he was too busy conning the boat to feel fear. At any rate, he appeared remarkably calm. And yet, there was no doubt that a destroyer was on his tail. Was this where it would all end? Would this daring raid end here in the destruction of his boat, his crew, and himself?

The fast destroyer could easily overtake him, but the destroyer captain was confused. He did not see any boat ahead of him, and he was misled by false clues. On the bridge of the U-47 the astonished Prien saw the ship turn away and search in another direction, and later in the distance he heard it dropping depth charges.

Reaching the narrow channel again, Prien threaded his way through the obstacles. It was now low tide, and the current was against him. For a time he made no progress, and then, at full speed, he passed the southern blockships and with great relief arrived in the open sea. Miraculously, they were out. The U-47 had entered the lion's den and escaped without harm to a single member of the crew. The perfectionist Prien wrote in his log, "The helmsman does magnificently." Eager to share the good news, Prien said, "Pass the word, we're through." The crew let out a spontaneous cheer, and they sailed happily homeward.

Before the attack, the crew, probably trying to reassure themselves, had passed around a cartoon of a bull with its head down and nostrils smoking. It reminded them of their commander whom they called "Harry Hotspur." During the relatively easy return trip, Endrass had a flash of genius. He put some of the more artistic members of the crew to work painting a ferocious bull on the conning tower. The U-47 had a new name: Bull of Scapa Flow.

Entering the harbor at Wilhelmshaven, Prien noticed that the security was no better than at Scapa Flow. The British, he thought, could make a similar attack on them. But this was a time for a joyous welcome. Prien and his crew became the heroes of the hour. There was no doubt about the triumph. The British had somberly announced on the radio that the *Royal Oak* had been sunk. They also reported that the attacking U-boat had been sent to the bottom. Now this crew of alleged ghosts arrived to a tumultuous greeting, and Prien's name became a household word throughout the Third Reich.

As the boat tied up, Raeder and Doenitz were all smiles as they waited on the dock. Raeder, chief of the German navy, called the Kriegsmarine, went on board at once, shook hands with each member of the crew, and on the spot awarded each one of them the Iron Cross, Second Class. Prien received the Iron Cross, First Class. But that was not their only recognition. The fuehrer himself wanted to honor and glorify these brave sailors, and they were all flown to

U-251 ties up at Narvik, Norway, in June 1942. (PHOTO: U.S. NAVY)

Berlin that same day. The overjoyed Hitler greeted the men in the Reich Chancellery, and Prien received an even higher decoration, the Knight's Cross of the Iron Cross. It was jubilation day for Adolf Hitler and the German people. The shame of Scapa Flow had been replaced by an extraordinary victory.

For all of the fanfare, there was a deeper significance to Prien's achievement. It meant a new day for the German U-boat. During World War I, the U-boat had been a menace to the Allies, but not a decisive factor in the war. After the war, German submarines were outlawed by the Treaty of Versailles.

It was not until 1935 that Hitler openly ignored the treaty that ended the first war and started to build U-boats. Even then, however, submariners did not believe that they received the recognition they deserved. The submarine service was really a backwater in the navy, and there was competition for attention from other branches of the armed forces. All eyes seemed to be on Hermann Goering and his new, glamorous Luftwaffe. Air power was commonly believed to be the weapon to win the next war for the Germans. Besides, Hitler, a corporal in World War I, was more comfortable with the army and air force. He admitted his lack of understanding of the navy and once said, "On land I am a hero, at sea I am a coward."

Now, after Scapa Flow, the submarine service was looked upon in a different light. If submariners did not get everything they wanted, they had at least achieved greater respect and brighter prospects for the future.

Following Prien's attack, Karl Doenitz received a promotion to rear admiral with more authority as the flag officer commanding submarines. With more power he was confident that he could make the U-boat arm a major force in bringing about the downfall of the Allies.

During World War I, Doenitz had been a young submarine officer who was devoted to the service. The challenge intrigued him. He liked the opportunity to stand on his own feet and to perform duties that required skill and courage. He once wrote, "I was fascinated by that unique spirit of comradeship engendered by destiny and hardship shared in the community of a U-boat crew, where every man's well-being was in the hands of all and where every single man was an indispensable part of the whole."

Doenitz had come close to death in U-boats, but he never lost his fascination with them. During World War I, while commanding a U-boat off Sicily, he sighted a convoy and submerged to make a daylight attack. But things did not go smoothly. A basic fault in the longitudinal stability of the boat caused the crew practically to stand on their heads. The batteries spilled, the lights went out, and the boat dropped down into the deep sea. Theoretically, the boat could not descend more than about 200 feet. Attempts to stop their steep descent failed. Doenitz ordered the tanks blown to lighten the boat and went full astern with the rudder hard over, but it kept going down and down until they reached about 300 feet. Then, as the end seemed near, the boat was light enough to start up. Doenitz said, "Like a stick plunged under water and then suddenly released, it shot upwards and out of the water, to arrive with a crash on the surface."

Worse still, the boat surfaced in the middle of the enemy convoy, and the armed guard on the merchant ships started to fire on the boat. Doenitz had exhausted his compressed air and could not dive again. He was trapped, and the boat started sinking. There was no alternative except to abandon ship.

Seven men were lost, but Allied destroyers picked up the rest of the crew, and Doenitz spent the remainder of the war in a British prison camp where he had time to think about submarine tactics. He came to the conclusion then that a number of U-boats making a simultaneous attack on a convoy would have a better chance of success. It was an idea that he would not forget.

After the first war, Doenitz remained in the small German navy, but since there were no submarines, he spent most of his time on surface ships. In 1935, much to his surprise, he received orders to form a new U-boat arm. Despite his previous attachment, he was not pleased with the orders at the time because U-boats then seemed like an unimportant, forgotten part of the navy with little future.

Discouraged or not, Doenitz cast his doubts aside and went to work with a will. In the years after the war a handful of men had kept their faith in the U-boat and worked secretly on new, improved designs. By June 1935 they had constructed under the strictest security the first submarine of the Nazi era. It was designated U-1 and was rapidly followed by eleven similar boats. They were small, only 250 tons, but they were easy to handle and included many engineering improvements over the primitive World War I boats. Soon the little boats would be affectionately called canoes. This was the beginning of the new U-boat arm that Doenitz led.

The U-boat leader quietly gathered a few top-notch men around him. One of his chief aides was "Papa" Thedsen who had started in the navy as a lowly stoker and had risen to engineer admiral. Doenitz's interest was in ability, not aristocracy. He wanted men he could depend on, men who shared his enthusiasm for U-boats. Professionalism was important, but Doenitz firmly believed that that alone was not enough. He brought together men with spirit and dedication, men who were fascinated by this strange world of life under water.

In the few years before war broke out again, Doenitz carried out an intense training program. Every man had to be an expert at his job. There was no room for error, and officers drilled into recruits' minds that each man's life depended on the other crewmen.

Doenitz, in contrast to the Prussian Raeder, was not an aloof commander. He became personally acquainted with the men under him and listened to their ideas. Personal contact, Doenitz believed, was an important element of leadership. His attitude made him popular with his men, but there was no question that he was the officer in charge. He was a disciplinarian who demanded top performance. Those who slacked off on the job or did not have the temperament for the submarine service received orders elsewhere. Every man was a volunteer, and there was never a shortage of volunteers. Esprit de corps was high.

Even with professionalism and enthusiasm, plenty of obstacles remained to be overcome. Problems of design, construction, training, and tactics all multiplied. And Germany had to overcome many basic disadvantages to become a serious naval power. Unlike Great Britain, the German nation was a part of the land mass of Central Europe with difficult access to the high seas. Great Britain blocked the North Sea, which was Germany's best entrance into the Atlantic Ocean. And a southern route through the English Channel could be easily blocked by the British in wartime. There was a narrow passage between the Shetland Islands and Norway, but this was a hazardous voyage, especially with the advent of longer-range aircraft. At least U-boats could submerge on their way to the Atlantic.

The first U-boats were too small to operate in the Atlantic. A larger boat was needed, not as large, however, as some officers in the high command wanted. Naval officers traditionally dreamed of bigger warships, and some saw possibilities for a huge 2,000-ton boat. But Doenitz differed. He knew that the war-making power of a submarine did not necessarily increase with the boat's size. He saw size as a hindrance because a big boat would need more time to dive, have more difficulty surfacing, and be more complex to handle while submerged. It would be slower, clumsier, and a bigger target.

Eventually, Doenitz had his way, and a Type VII boat
with various modifications became more or less standard.
There would be other types, larger and smaller, but this
was the boat that carried the major burden during World
War II. This was the boat that would menace the Allies and
that was on station from the first to the last day of the war.

Hitler steadfastly claimed that he would not go to war
with Great Britain. Doenitz was skeptical. He saw Great
Britain as the probable enemy in the next war and strongly
believed that the U-boat would be the decisive weapon in
winning the war. With hundreds of boats, Germany could
strangle that isolated island nation. The critical element in
the war would be the destruction of Allied shipping. It
would be a battle of tonnage. The aim was to send tons and
tons of British ships to the bottom, cut off food, fuel, and
other vital imports, and force the nation to surrender. It
could be quite simple.

Nevertheless, while Doenitz may have been right in his
estimate of the situation, Hitler and others in high places
were not willing to appropriate money and materials before
the war to build hundreds of U-boats. Doenitz wanted to
start the war with three hundred boats.

On September 3, 1939, the day Great Britain and France
declared war on Germany, Doenitz had forty-six boats ready
for action and a total of fifty-six commissioned. Of the forty-
six available boats, only twenty-two could fight in the Atlantic. The others were small 250-ton craft that were suitable
only for action in the North Sea because of their limited
range. Because of logistical and other problems, only five
to seven boats could operate in the Atlantic at one time.
For all of Hitler's braggadocio, the war began for the Third
Reich with a poorly equipped U-boat arm, and no one
realized this more clearly than Doenitz.

The U-boats had other limitations. Submariners were to
abide by international law that from a military standpoint
seemed ridiculous. The 1936 London Submarine Agree-

ment placed all kinds of handicaps on them. Among other things, a U-boat could not make a submerged attack on a merchant ship, and before attacking had to see to the safety of the merchant crew by endangering themselves. Yet Hitler wanted this agreement strictly enforced, not for humane reasons, but in the political hope that he could negotiate peace with the French and British.

With these disadvantages, the war began with a blunder for the U-boats on the first day of World War II. Despite clear instructions to the contrary, the impulsive twenty-six-year-old commander of U-30, Fritz-Ludwig Lemp, sighted a large, blacked-out ship zigzagging on a strange route. He quickly identified it as a British auxiliary cruiser, dived, and fired a salvo of torpedoes that hit the target with an enormous explosion. He had struck the passenger liner *Athenia*. It took on a list and started to sink. On board were 1,400 persons, many of them women and children. Some were immediately killed, others were trapped below, and still others, in a state of shock, tried to round up children or save themselves.

The ship did not sink at once, and the curious Lemp, under cover of darkness, came to the surface to see what he had accomplished. Standing off about half a mile, he commenced firing with his guns to destroy the ship's wireless antenna. As he watched the action and took a careful look at the enemy, he realized that he had disobeyed his orders. He decided he had better escape fast, and he made no effort to help his desperate victims.

The next morning, the *Athenia* was still afloat, but its fate was certain. Circling the ship were lifeboats filled with anxious survivors. They were picked up by a Norwegian freighter and later by two destroyers, the American merchant ship, *City of Flint*, and a yacht, *Southern Cross*. In all they saved 1,300 persons, but 118 lost their lives, including 22 Americans.

The incident intensified the tension between the United States and Germany and enraged the British press, which described the affair as an "atrocity." The guilty Lemp did not report the action, and Doenitz, unaware of it, denied any part in the shabby event. In response to the British outcry, the perplexed Germans, under the influence of their propaganda chief, Joseph Goebbels, claimed that Winston Churchill had intentionally committed sabotage to provoke a frightful charge against Germany.

Late in September, Lemp returned to base at Wilhelmshaven and personally reported his part in the action to Doenitz. By this time there could be no public admission of guilt, and Lemp was sworn not to reveal what had happened.

The chastened Lemp was let off easily. He was placed under arrest for one day and then returned to sea where he remained an aggressive commander. Hitler, however, was infuriated. For political reasons he did not want to draw any more countries into the war. He issued stricter instructions to prevent attacks on passenger liners even if they were escorted by warships. French ships were exempt from all attacks except in self-defense. For U-boat commanders this was like fighting with their hands tied behind their backs.

Under these restrictions, the U-boat commanders did their best. In the early days of the war, they were professional sailors, not ardent Nazis, and many of them let their better instincts come to the fore. More than one Allied survivor reported that U-boats approached their lifeboats and offered food, water, or medicine and gave them a course to the nearest shore. One brash commander, Herbert Schulze, sent a radio message to Winston Churchill, then first lord of the Admiralty: "Have sunk British S.S. *Firby*. . . . Please pick up the crew."

In the first few weeks of war things often went awry.

Targets were missed or torpedoes failed to explode, and yet there were some remarkable successes. One day in September, Kapitänleutnant Otto Schuhart, patrolling a shipping lane west of the English Channel in the U-29 sighted a British aircraft carrier in his periscope. The carrier was a long way off, but Schuhart slowly worked his way closer. The carrier zigzagged, but the submarine kept a parallel course. Finally, the carrier turned about seventy degrees, and the perspiring Schuhart, facing the sun, made a quick guess rather than a careful calculation and fired his torpedoes. He knew destroyers were escorting the carrier so he immediately started to dive deeper while the torpedoes ran their course. On the way down, two thunderous explosions were so close that Schuhart thought his boat was hit. He went deeper and found to his surprise that the boat had not suffered any damage. Before the war, commanders had orders not to go below 150 feet. Schuhart was now at 250 feet. Could the boat take the pressure? Schuhart did not know, but he soon discovered that the depth did not cause problems.

Listening intently, the crew heard propellers. The destroyers must have been on top of them. Four depth charges shook the boat roughly. Schuhart, hiding his true feelings, calmly issued orders that gave the crew confidence. For hours the depth charges continued. Then near midnight, the attacks stopped and there was quiet. Schuhart surfaced and radioed his good news back to base. In twenty-four hours all Germany learned that the British aircraft carrier *Courageous* had been sunk with the loss of more than five hundred men.

Schuhart's success was outstanding, and in German eyes he was a hero. Yet the submarine service still received little recognition. Hitler was not completely convinced of the boats' value for devastation. It was not until Prien entered and escaped from Scapa Flow that the public's imagination, and Hitler's, was captured. From that time on a new attitude prevailed. More money and materials became available. A construction program began in earnest, and the U-boat war gained momentum.

After Scapa Flow, international law was forgotten. Soon Hitler permitted the torpedoing of merchant ships without warning, and in another month there were no restrictions against attacking passenger ships. The death struggle to strangle the Allies was on.

2

U-BOAT LIFE

The handsome, blond Kapitänleutnant Joachim Schepke had a flair for the dramatic, and he was quite willing to play the part of the hero. His qualifications for the role, however, went far beyond mere affectation. They were based on skill and solid seamanship. His charming, carefree manner hid his intense ferocity in carrying the war to the enemy.

During the winter of 1939–40 there was little military action on land. It was the time of the so-called phony war when some people on both sides deluded themselves into thinking that the war would soon peter out and reasonable men would come to terms. At sea, men like Schepke led the U-boat war, and it was far from phony. The attacks continued without quarter.

The bitter cold winter offered some solace for the submariners as they circled Great Britain. Mean weather provided low visibility as U-boats laid mines in British harbors and waited offshore to torpedo arriving or departing merchant ships.

Off the coast during this dreary winter, the temperature inside Schepke's little "canoe," the U-19, hovered around zero degrees Fahrenheit. Heat was scarce in U-boats. It wasted electricity. Only summer or southern waters provided warmth, and then it was too much.

Schepke ignored the cold and forgot all about discomfort when he sighted an enemy destroyer. He attacked, but this was not to be a day of glory. The torpedo missed the target and blew up on the shore. The explosion gave the sub away, and the destroyer rushed toward the U-19. At that instant, Schepke ordered, "Dive," and to hurry the descent further he ordered the crew to rush forward to the bow to add all their weight. On the way down, despite the extra weight forward, the aft dropped and the bow rose. Quickly, all ballast tanks were flooded, and the U-boat started down again and ended up on the bottom with a violent smash that stunned everyone.

The depth charges from the destroyer began to detonate. Some exploded so close to the U-19 that the paint peeled off the bulkheads, instruments broke, and compressed air escaped. At times the lights went off, and the darkness increased the crew's sense of helplessness. Yet Schepke played his part well. He continued to look confident and unconcerned while his men waited, hoped, and prayed in their claustrophobic hell. The slightest sign of fear could have sent panic sweeping through the boat like wildfire.

The depth charges continued. Men tossed about from the blows, and they saw the bulkheads begin to buckle. The hull could not take much more. The barrels of TNT dropped by destroyers to explode at a set depth rarely hit their target with a bull's-eye. If the charge blew up within ten or twenty feet, the boat would probably be destroyed. Most U-boats, instead, were lost as a result of the total damage inflicted by a number of nearby explosions.

Finally, Schepke said to his chief engineer, "Let's get out of here." As the boat started its ascent, nothing seemed to work right. Abnormal sounds throughout the boat were signs of a variety of damages. Yet slowly it rose, and the depth charges became more distant.

In the gray light of dawn, the U-19 rose to periscope depth. Schepke could easily see the shore, but there were no warships in view. He surfaced, recharged the batteries, and life became almost normal. Memories were short. Once the depth charging was over, the anxiety did not linger. Remembrance of the ordeal, like the memory of pain, faded. They had survived and soon would be in search of prey again.

For Schepke and his fellow commanders, to experience a near fatal attack on the bottom and then to surface with the probability that the enemy lay in wait took rare fortitude. And to remain calm and never show the slightest flicker of fear demanded an almost unnatural degree of self-possession.

One mystery of human nature is why anyone wanted to spend a large part of life beneath the sea in confined, miserable conditions. Even in peacetime the submarine service was filled with dangers. During a war, the chances for survival were slim. Yet men were intrigued by the challenge.

Karl Doenitz never regretted his U-boat service. He believed that he understood its magnetic appeal. He wrote, "It gave me everything in life that a man who is a man can desire—responsibility, success, failure, the loyalty and respect of other men, the need to find oneself, and adversity." That satisfied him.

Nevertheless, it took a special kind of man to put up with a life that at times was almost unbearable. Life in any submarine required self-control under severe circumstances. Life in a German Type VII submarine was much worse. The vessel was smaller than the Japanese I-boat or the American submarines of World War II. The German designers under the influence of Doenitz disregarded what most men considered minimal comforts. There was only one reason to build a U-boat: to make war. Nothing else mattered to him.

Seamen at work on U-86 during the summer of 1942. (PHOTO: BUNDESARCHIV)

Propagandists may have tried to glamorize the service, but recruits soon found out that they led a Spartan life of rigid discipline and training. Perfection in performance may have been unattainable, but hard taskmasters strained to reach that goal. On a submarine there was little margin for error. The technical requirements were tough; the human requirements were tougher. If, as the old saying goes, familiarity breeds contempt, U-boat men should have held each other in contempt. Submariners could not escape one another's company, and yet they managed to work and play together, and they were well aware that they might die together.

The Germans called submarines of all nations U-boats. It was short for *Unterseeboot* (undersea boat). The Allies, however, referred only to German submarines as U-boats, and to them, as Winston Churchill said, the term had a villainous ring while Allied submarines sounded more virtuous.

The U-boat was built to present as small a target as possible. It was a weapon of stealth, and the less seen the better. Unlike the Italian submarine, it had a small conning tower so that its silhouette on the sea would be negligible. During the war, the Type VII had a displacement on the surface of 600 to 1,000 tons, and a surface speed of 16 to 17 knots. Underwater, the speed was almost 8 knots. A speedy underwater boat would have been the answer to a German submariner's dream, but no one had the technical knowledge to build such a boat at the time.

Surprisingly, the World War II U-boat, despite its name, was not designed as a true underwater boat. Most of the time, or at least as much of the time as possible, the boat remained on the surface, because the commander could see more from the bridge than through the periscope. Beneath periscope level the boat was completely blind, and the only hint that an enemy ship was nearby came to the hydrophone operator listening for propeller noises.

One of the main reasons the boats did not remain underwater for long was the need to recharge the batteries for the electric motors that drove the boat when they were below. The crew needed breathing space for that job.

Doenitz regarded the U-boat as a diving vessel. It could dive to disappear from the enemy, and that was its unique advantage. Diving time was always critical, and training exercises were endless to cut the time to a minimum. The Type VII could be taken down in as few as twenty seconds. That happened only when conditions were ideal, however. In varying situations the dive might take precious minutes.

What makes such a boat dive? The principle is simple. Add weight and the boat will go down like a stone. Reduce weight and the boat will rise. Between an inner and outer hull are ballast tanks with holes in the bottom. When the boat dives, the tanks are flooded with water to a set level. The boat is held at the desired level by vanes, or hydroplanes, on each side. They move up or down, just as the steering rudder moves from side to side. Underwater, the boat has to keep moving or it will drop to the bottom. When the commander gives the order to surface, seamen standing by valves in the control room inject compressed air into the tanks to force the water out at the bottom, and the bow and stern planes lift the boat as do the wings of an airplane.

In tight maneuvering, especially when firing torpedoes, an alert planesman continually had to adjust the angle of the planes to keep the boat steady. At the same time, care had to be taken with the balance of the forward and auxiliary tanks. It was an exact process to maintain a level by blowing or flooding the tanks. When the torpedoes were ready to fire, the tubes were flooded first, and then the bow or stern doors opened.

The torpedoes were intricate weapons that operated like small submarines, except that they were faster. They had a range of four or five miles and could reach a speed of 30 knots. Before each firing they were set for speed, course, and depth.

The delicate torpedoes, called "eels" by the crew, were often troublesome and disappointing. Torpedo mechanics nursed these temperamental weapons with the utmost care. Although the electric torpedoes no longer gave themselves away with a broad wake as the air-propelled torpedoes did during World War I, they were often erratic in behavior, especially in the early part of the war. The electric torpedo was probably the most reliable at first, but the firing pistol

Loading a torpedo on board a German U-boat. In the foreground is
an 88-mm. gun. (PHOTO: U.S. NAVY)

was often defective. At the start, most torpedoes exploded on contact. Later, magnetic torpedoes that exploded when they reached a magnetic field caused by a ship's steel hull were common. In time, other improvements were made in various types. One could be set to zigzag or circle after running a certain distance, and an acoustic torpedo could home in on the noise of a ship's propeller.

When a commander sighted his prey at a distance, his tactic was to place his boat ahead of the moving target. Torpedoes took time to run their course, and the chances of hitting the mark were better when the boat lay ahead of a ship rather than behind it. Firing a torpedo astern might end in failure because it could not catch up before it wore out and sank. To place a boat favorably in the crosswires of the periscope took time and patience. Sometimes the pursuit took days.

To reach a favorable position, submarines went full speed on the surface as long as possible. The chase was always exciting, and everyone was on his toes. This was what they had waited for—action. The commander, on the bridge, continually looked through his powerful binoculars for any signs of interference. He wanted no surprises.

Below, the torpedomen stood by. A petty officer operated the range finder, and an officer worked at an attack table. The crew members made calculations for the attack, rapidly figuring the speed of the target, the range, the speed and running depth of the torpedo. Firing was never simple, and the crew left as little as possible to chance. They had to aim the torpedo at a spot in the ocean ahead of the enemy ship, and to do so they needed an estimate of the target's speed and course. The commander was continually advised of the calculations and gave the decisive orders from the bridge or, when submerged, from the conning tower or control room. When satisfied, he called out, *"Achtung"* (attention), and then "Fire when ready."

In an instant the torpedo officer replied, "Ready." Then there was another pause while a crewman made a final check to be sure that the target was in the crosswires. In seconds, the torpedo officer cried out, "Fire," and pressed a button. The petty officer in the torpedo room repeated the order, and the gunner's mate pulled the firing lever.

Everyone on board felt and heard the torpedo leave the boat. There was a tremble and a hissing sound. The commander and hydrophone operator timed the run while the crew anxiously waited for the sound of an explosion. If the boat immediately dived after firing, the commander was the only man who might see the action through the periscope. Throughout the action he kept the crew as well informed as he could. If the hit was a success and they did not find themselves pursued, the commander might let some of the men take a look through the periscope.

The sight they saw might be a raging fire on a tanker, a freighter breaking up, or passengers and crew running haphazardly for lifeboats. A sinking sent a wave of elation through the boat. No one thought of the inhumanity of such acts. Minds and consciences ignored the cruelty. It was kill or be killed, and they had done their job. The time was for celebration, not mourning. They could return to base with pride.

Sometimes a curious commander approached the lifeboats and asked their destination or inquired about the injured. Sometimes he apologized for the inconvenience and blamed it on the war. And sometimes he offered medicine, food, or water. Only in face-to-face encounters did a sense of sympathy arise for the victims, and an occasional humane act placed the war on a personal level. All other times it was an impersonal affair with no room for sentiment.

Sailing into port after a successful patrol was the best reward for any crew. White pennants flew from the periscope showing the number of merchant tons sunk. If a warship was sunk, the crew ran up a red banner. Exhilaration was in the air. They were met by a brass band, and very often by Doenitz, who eagerly awaited the latest news. He worried about his men and was always delighted to see them return and to share their success. When his men won decorations, Doenitz made a practice of distributing them at once. He recognized the psychological importance of immediate rewards, and he wanted the men, during their brief leaves, to show off what they had achieved. He knew that there might not be a next time.

Before the crews went on leave there was usually a party on board the boat, and all rank was obliterated while they enjoyed themselves. The "beer report," a tradition in the German navy, was the high point of the evening when the boners, or alleged boners, committed by each member during the cruise were humorously reviewed with broad exaggeration in a pseudo-serious way. No one, from the commander to the youngest seaman, escaped the barbs. Their common experience had formed a strong bond of comradeship.

Soon the jubilant crews were at sea again. As the war went on, the boats were forced to remain underwater for longer and longer periods of time. Convoy escorts increased, and Allied air power spread out over the Atlantic until there was little safety on the surface. Modifications were made to the boats so that they could stay submerged longer, and by the end of the war one boat did not surface for an incredible sixty-six days. Admittedly, the last days of that desperate cruise were horrible.

The Type VII boat was 220 feet long and 20 feet wide. Almost always the gray boats were described as cigar-shaped, and that is probably as good a description as any. Sometimes the boats were mistaken for whales, or whales for U-boats. On the surface the boat could cover about 6,200 miles, barely enough to cross the Atlantic and return.

Submerged, the distance was only 80 miles. The limited fuel capacity was a major drawback. Each boat had storage for only 67 tons of diesel fuel for cruising on the surface.

On the slippery deck there was usually one 3.5-inch gun mounted forward and a one-pound antiaircraft gun on the conning tower plus one or more 20-millimeter machine guns. After surfacing, gunners rushed through the conning tower hatch to take their positions as quickly as possible. In the beginning of the war aircraft were not considered much of a threat. Later more antiaircraft guns, both 20- and 37-millimeter, were added.

Lookouts stood guard forward and at the stern. On the bridge, exposed to the elements, were the watch officer, a boatswain's mate, and two or three other enlisted men. Ever-vigilant commanders were also there most of the time, scanning the sea for smoke or masts on the horizon.

In the bow compartment below there were four torpedo tubes, and in the stern, one tube. The torpedo officer, mechanics, and mates tended these tubes. The boats carried twelve to fourteen torpedoes to do their damage. Sometimes the torpedoes were replaced with mines that the men could launch through the tubes. Between the two ends of the boat the only passageway was a center aisle that ran through each compartment.

An enlisted man could not even claim a bunk of his own. The lower-ratings slept in shifts in their quarters in the forecastle at the forward end and took turns with bunks that were always "hot." Personal belongings were pitifully few because of the lack of space. Everything was cramped on board. The 40 or so men on the U-boat were more crowded than the 110 men on an American submarine of that time.

For meals, a portable table was placed in the passage between the lower bunks on each side where the men sat. While they ate, the upper bunks were folded away.

Abaft was the officers' wardroom, but officers did not fare much better than the men. Rank had few privileges as far as living conditions were concerned. At one end of the little wardroom the commander had his private cabin. To call it a cabin is misleading, however. A curtain simply concealed a part of the wardroom. The commander's quarters, however, were close to the heart of the boat. Nearby were the radio operator, the navigator, and the hydrophone operator.

The radio operator, a vital link to the outside world, could receive some messages when the boat was not submerged too deeply. But to send a message it was necessary to surface or raise an antenna above the sea, and there was always the danger of giving away the boat's location.

The navigator, as one might expect, held a key post. Unlike such officers on surface ships, he was often unable to "shoot the stars" and fix the boat's position, so he frequently navigated by dead reckoning. That meant he calculated the course by figuring time, speed, and distance. It was high-class guesswork, but certainly not a new method at sea. Columbus found his way across the Atlantic that way. As the war advanced, the underwater instruments improved and the navigator was aided by radar and other electronic equipment.

The hydrophone operator used his apparatus to listen for the sound of a ship's propeller that might indicate the presence of an enemy ship. His ear was well attuned to the noises of the deep, and he learned to make fine distinctions between ships and fishes.

Amidships, in the superstructure that rose from the deck were the conning tower and the hatch that gave access to the bridge. In the conning tower, the commander often operated a small, slim, attack periscope. With him were the helmsman and a torpedo director. A second periscope was used for reconnaissance. These optical wonders made

A U-boat commander using his periscope. (PHOTO: BUNDESARCHIV)

up of prisms and lenses were encased in tubes about 40 feet long. They magnified the scene above and could be raised or lowered by hydraulic power.

Beneath the conning tower was the control room. There, the German commander, unlike his American counterpart, frequently sat rather than stood at the periscope as he searched for targets and issued orders when the boat was submerged. The surrounding area was filled with wheels, valves, and levers that required experienced hands to operate. The wrong twist of a valve could cause disaster. Dials and pointers told the course, speed, and depth of the boat. When the boat dived, the commander and the chief engineer were in the control room. With them were the diving-rudder operators. When the diving alarm went off, every second counted. In a crash dive, the engine-room crews shut down the diesels and turned on the electric motors in an instant. In rapid succession, almost simultaneously, valves were opened to flood the tanks and the boat started downward. Speed was essential, but so was careful teamwork.

Astern of the control room were the petty officers' mess, more bunks, a crowded galley the size of a small closet where the cook was expected to prepare wholesome meals each day, and the engine room, which contained two diesel engines and two electric motors with banks of heavy storage batteries. Then there was the stern torpedo tube. On the surface the noisy diesel engines made a continual racket. The electric motors for running submerged were much quieter. Nevertheless, the deep had its own special noises, and there were plenty of eerie sounds when underwater.

The engineering officer, aided by a chief diesel mechanic and a chief electrical mechanic continually fretted and fumed over their engines. They and their men knew every part, and if the lights went out during an attack they were able to carry on in the dark. The lower ratings who worked in the engine room were called stokers, an old-fashioned term, even though they had no coal to stoke for a furnace.

The air pressure inside the hull was about the same as in the atmosphere. Outside the hull, the sea pressure depended on the boat's depth. If the boat went down to 500 feet, the sea pressure was 16 tons per square foot of surface. The boat had to be well built to withstand these pressures.

If you served on a U-boat you had to make up your mind

to ignore foul air, dampness, and strong smells. The smells were all kinds. They came from the bilges, food, and fuel. The close proximity to the diesel engines was enough to sicken many stout stomachs. The food was the best quality in the navy, but at the start of a voyage it was stacked everywhere, and as time went on some usually spoiled. Before long, the loaves of bread took on a furry greenish mildew, and the crew called them white rabbits. At best, cooking fumes from the tiny galley mixed with the other vapors were hardly easy on the nose.

The worst odors probably came from the men themselves as the days turned into weeks. Washing was another luxury restricted by space. Water storage was limited. Even drinking water was rationed. Officers used fresh water sparsely, lower ratings had the unpleasant experience of washing in harsh seawater that dried their skin and never left anyone feeling clean. As time wore on, personal cleanliness became nonexistent. It did not help the crewmen appreciate their shipmates.

Privacy was unknown. Perhaps one advantage of lack of space was the absence of a brig into which to throw an errant crew member. Misbehavior did not go unpunished, but it was a challenge for the commander to think of original ways to punish the offender. Many officers were reluctant to place men on report when they returned to base. By then, the misconduct might be forgotten, and besides, returning home was a time for rejoicing. They preferred to discipline during a cruise, and the question was always how.

One imaginative commander, Wolfgang Lüth, meted out such punishments as three days of sleeping on deck without a mattress or blanket instead of three days in a cell. He also announced each sentence to the entire crew. Most men wanted to avoid this humiliation.

Commanders had another challenge: keeping their men

occupied. It was not easy. The moments of action were far fewer than the days of monotony, and a bored crew could cause trouble. Organized work routines helped, yet the men could not be expected to work continually. And smoking cigarettes on deck or drinking coffee in their off time only frayed their nerves and damaged their stomachs. They also tired of one another's often-repeated stories about escapades ashore.

Days and nights ran together on a submarine and increased the abnormality of life. Lüth did his best to create a distinction between day and night, weekdays and Sundays. At supper, he dimmed the lights, and for an hour after supper he conducted a gramophone concert. On Sundays he always started the day with the same record. It went, "Till ten o'clock it's my Sunday treat to stay in bed and rest my feet." The last Sunday record was "Abendlied," sung by the choirboys of Regensburg Cathedral.

To give a further sense of time, Lüth doled out newspapers and magazines that he had taken aboard like a miser. Regardless of the date, the crew eagerly read them all. Books were another high-value item, and the men read and reread them.

Effective commanders knew that entertainment was psychologically important. The men needed some kind of mental escape from the ever-present strains. Sometimes the amusement simply created idle conversation or a laugh. One commander with a sense of humor brought a bowl of goldfish on board and named each of the fish after an Allied leader. When "Winston Churchill" died, it was placed in a test tube and pickled for everyone to see.

Lüth held a singing competition, and every single member of the crew had to perform before the microphone. It is easy to imagine some of the howls that must have gone up from the singers as well as the audience. Although they may not have produced any opera stars, such activities

provided fun and relaxation. Cards and chess were good
time killers, and some crews held tournaments. Other times,
officers conducted lectures on popular subjects to rouse
interest.

Lüth was a thoughtful commander. He cared about his
men, and he was wise enough to know that while all decisions were his, the slightest error by any man could spoil
an attack or sink the boat. When he punished someone, he
was quick to show that he did not hold a grudge. That same
man, he knew, would be needed another time.

Men performing the same dangerous duties every day
showed an odd quirk of human behavior: they became
indifferent or careless about risk. A good commander could
not relax rigid standards of safety. High performance
depended on discipline. At the same time, as Lüth advised
others, commanders should always be even tempered and
approachable. An aloof or resentful commander might not
receive a critical piece of information from a suppressed
crew member. Sometimes Lüth was disappointed, yet he
continued to trust his men.

The U-boat crews were all young. Most of the lower-
rated men were twenty to twenty-two years old, and petty
officers were rarely older than twenty-five. The officers
were also young, and before the war ended at least one
commander was only twenty-one. Submarine warfare was
a young man's game. These men, not much more than
boys, created an undersea terror and struck fear in the
hearts of the enemy. In their innocence and ignorance, they
nobly served an ignoble cause.

3

THE ACES

Otto Kretschmer was a man who loved a good cigar as much as he hated idle conversation. It was no wonder his men called him Silent Otto. Unlike Lüth, he was naturally aloof and often stood off to one side of the bridge quietly puffing his cigar and mulling over his next move. In his white covered cap that only commanders wore and leather coat, with binoculars strapped around his neck, he made a lonely figure as he watched for the slightest sign of action. Modern mechanical gadgets were fine, but he was a true seaman who believed in using his eyes. And when he spoke, he expected to be obeyed. No crew member ever made the mistake of thinking that the close confines of the boat made Kretschmer a person with whom they might take liberties.

Kretschmer's bearing announced that he was a man of precision who set high standards and expected others to meet them. He did not need words. When he boarded the boat at the outset of a patrol, he appeared in an immaculate uniform. There was nothing careless about his appearance. When he returned to base, he performed the more difficult task of again wearing a perfectly cleaned and pressed uniform.

Doenitz was aware of Kretschmer's devotion to duty before the war and had made him a U-boat commander when he was only twenty-four. Now that war had begun, Kretschmer knew that his great opportunity had arrived. He had no intention of missing that chance through negligence or someone else's weakness.

In the early days of the war Kretschmer sailed close to the British coast and successfully laid mines and torpedoed his first ship. It would not be his last. Before long his crew realized that they were sailing with a lucky commander. But what was luck? Was it Kretschmer's grim intolerance of anything less than perfection? Whatever it was, good luck was an important companion for every U-boat. Some boats seemed to have it, real or imagined, while others did not. The commander was the key. Some had a knack for success.

U-boat crews knew that victorious moments were rare and defeats were frequent. When they returned to base, stories circulated among them about the lucky and the unlucky. They heard about the commander of U-39 who sighted the huge aircraft carrier, *Ark Royal*, took aim, and fired his torpedoes. The attack should have been a feather in his cap. Instead, the torpedoes missed and exploded in the carrier's wake. The noise signaled the destroyer screen and the carrier crew sent the U-39 to the bottom with all hands lost. U-boat men did not like to hear such stories, but they always made the rounds.

Although Kretschmer seemed to make his own luck, the war did not always go his way. One night he sighted his first convoy. He was in a good position to attack and without wasting any time fired all of his torpedoes at a steady stream

Captain Otto Kretschmer. (PHOTO: BUNDESARCHIV-MILITARCHIV)

of targets and then dived. He probably sank one ship, but that was much less than he had hoped for.

At a depth of about 100 feet, Kretschmer ordered the boat trimmed and leveled off. Then he found that he had not escaped detection. A new antisubmarine corvette was on his trail, and a powerful depth charge attack began. The men counted ten charges that badly shook the boat and shattered equipment.

Kretschmer decided to dive deeper. He went to 350 feet, cut the speed to a minimum, and waited for the corvette to lose interest in the search. He was disappointed. The attack continued relentlessly, and the depth charges kept dropping hour after hour. The air in the boat grew stale, and the crew put on their emergency masks to help purify the air they breathed.

Slowly the boat crept through the water as Kretschmer tried to evade the attackers. There seemed to be no escape. Wherever Kretschmer went, the British soon followed. For a brief spell there would be silence. Then the charges would start again. Each man remained as motionless as possible to save air and maintain quiet. At their stations or in their bunks they prayed, waited, and exerted every ounce of self-control. In such moments submariners always fought a mental war with their own inner thoughts. They battled for control of their fear.

Four, five, six hours went by without relief. As they waited, Kretschmer was the perfect example of the cool commander. He sat on the deck in the control room and casually read a book. His confidence calmed the crew and created the desired effect. As time passed, one younger officer noticed that the commander was not turning many pages. He sneaked a closer look and saw that the book was upside down.

Still more hours passed. Kretschmer worried about the batteries, which would soon need recharging. Without power the boat could sink to the bottom and be crushed in the depths. In six more hours, with every minute dragging, the boat had slowly slipped to a depth of well below 600 feet, which was beyond the safe level. Kretschmer had to act soon. He had to surface or sink. Yet he still waited as the air grew increasingly fetid. Soon they would suffocate.

Finally, the explosions were fewer and farther away. Early in the morning of the next day, after 127 depth charges and nineteen hours of agony, Kretschmer gave the order to surface. The enemy had disappeared, and the men climbed up the hatch, their entryway to a new life, and gulped in the fresh air. Kretschmer had done it again. They had survived.

Oddly enough, Kretschmer had a sense of humor despite his remoteness. On another patrol in the vicinity of the Shetland Islands, Kretschmer searched for the British fleet. It was a fruitless effort until a lookout shouted that he had sighted an enemy cruiser at anchor. Kretschmer spotted the sighting and went on the attack. He fired two torpedoes, and one found its mark with a crash. Then, too late, he learned that the "cruiser" was only a huge rock. Kretschmer was disgusted, but he did not keep his embarrassment a secret. Instead, he radioed headquarters that he had torpedoed, but not sunk, a rock.

The headquarters staff did not appreciate or understand Kretschmer's sense of humor. Then, to further confuse the situation, the British announced that H.M.S. *Nelson* had been damaged by a mine and, because the German word for rock is *felsen*, the Nazis concluded that Kretschmer had hit the British ship. It appeared to them to be a simple error of transmission. Fortunately, Kretschmer's explanation entertained Doenitz. The admiral might not have been so amused if he had not been aware that Kretschmer was one of his most able commanders. He knew that more would be heard from this young man.

The Atlantic was a big ocean in which a few small boats were expected to create havoc. The problem was always the same, to find the enemy. And to find the enemy in the wide expanses of the sea was not easy. U-boat crews spent much time waiting in anticipation in the most likely Allied shipping lanes. The Allies shifted their routes as much as possible, but the North Atlantic was still the busiest and most critical area.

Naval operations in the Atlantic were much different from those in the Pacific. No huge task forces confronted one another as at Midway or in the struggle for Guadalcanal and the Philippines. The brief forays of the battleships *Graf Spee* and *Bismarck* in the Atlantic ended in failure for the Germans, and no operation at sea was a massive array of opposing forces.

The solitary submarine bore the brunt for cutting Great Britain's lifeline in isolated actions. These were lonely encounters on the high seas, and many were lost to recorded history. For some, death came quickly, for others it came too slowly. Merchant sailors, gasping for breath in oil-laden waters, and submariners, slowly despairing in the depths, looked on death as their escape.

Propagandists on both sides shouted about their triumphs and remained as silent as possible about their losses. High commands merely added more numbers to their confidential statistical tables and tried to analyze whether they were winning or losing.

Doenitz had not forgotten his theory of *Rudeltaktik*, the tactic of attacking convoys with a swarm of boats. The trouble was that he did not have enough boats in 1939 and 1940, and he had to rely on the audacity of his individual commanders.

Despite the small number of boats, the early successes were encouraging. One reason was that the British, in the years between the wars, had underestimated the U-boat threat. The overconfident British officers believed that they had discovered the scientific answer to such a menace. They had developed asdic, a transmitter-receiver that sent sound waves through the water. When a sound wave ran into a submerged object, it bounced back to the sender. The transmission and echo made a "ping." This submarine-detection system seemed like the answer to their prayers. But they were wrong. Asdic was a step forward, but it had serious limitations and needed further improvement. And when a submarine was on the surface, asdic was useless.

Doenitz enjoyed the good news that reached him while he watched the exchange rate. Were the British ships worth the number of U-boats lost? That was always the big question. As he studied the numbers in the early days, he could only be pleased. Although he had lost men he had known and admired, he looked at the cold numbers. The rate was never static. Nonetheless, in the first few months the U-boats had sunk about twenty merchant ships for each boat lost. The lonely little boats had made a good beginning. The relatively ineffective asdic and the shortage of convoy escorts had made the British vulnerable.

As the tonnage sunk increased, the stars among the U-boat commanders began to emerge. The hotheaded Prien, hero of Scapa Flow, had already made a name for himself, and he continued to build an enviable record. Then Kretschmer joined him as a top ace.

The daring Schepke had been a friendly rival of Prien and Kretschmer since his earliest days in the U-boat service. Now he became known for his competence and clear head as much as for his charm. His record of sinkings grew until he had sunk thirty-nine ships that added up to 159,000 tons. He was the third man in a triumvirate of the Third Reich's greatest aces.

Still other aces came to the fore. The considerate Lüth proved to be a confident and successful commander, and then he was reported lost. The British announced that they had sunk his boat, and Doenitz accepted the story since there appeared to be confirmation. Too much time had elapsed since Lüth's last message. Days passed, and then the irrepressible commander surprised everyone by showing up.

Lüth had survived a deadly attack by fooling the British into thinking that his boat was sunk. The ruse worked only after the crew had endured long, agonizing hours on the bottom. Those without a duty to perform lay down in their bunks. Lüth told them to sleep so that they would use less air. But who could sleep? As the air supply dwindled, the crew put on oxygen masks. The trapped men made a weird scene. With masks over their faces they looked like monsters to one another. And yet, like Kretschmer's men, they lived through the ordeal. Soon Lüth was another ace who won the Knight's Cross with almonds. No Allied destroyer ever caught him, and yet his end was tragic. At the close of the war he was shot by mistake by a German sentry.

Another new ace was Herbert Schulze, commander of U-48, who was the first to sink 100,000 tons. Doenitz was proud of these men whom he had trained so carefully and given fatherly advice. They formed an elite circle and served the Third Reich well.

Thoughts of a "phony war" vanished in the spring of 1940. In lightning strikes, Hitler took over Denmark and Norway, and by June the Netherlands, Belgium, and France had fallen.

The Norwegian coast was an immediate concern for the U-boat arm in the brief battle there with the Allies. All boats were withdrawn from operations on the high seas and prepared to support the invasion of Norway. This was a chance to attack warships.

Prien was always in the center of action. The poor boy from Leipzig who had yearned for fame could not be accused of resting on his laurels. He had not forgotten his struggles as a young merchant marine officer and was making up for his years of poverty and obscurity. During the depression years before the war he had earned a master's license, but there had been no ships to command. As an alternative he worked in a voluntary Nazi labor camp and then joined the navy as an enlisted man. It had been a long, hard climb to his new eminence, and he had no intention of giving up now.

In mid-April, while patrolling in a Norwegian fjord, Prien peered through his periscope at a batch of Allied ships. This was better than Scapa Flow. He could disrupt the entire Allied force. With the skill for which he was known, Prien fired four torpedoes. Everything was in his favor, and yet he missed. He tried again and missed again. Lucky to get out alive, he returned to base a forlorn man.

Prien found that he was not alone in his misery. Others were equally unhappy even though they realized that success in wartime is never guaranteed. The golden opportunities that they had missed infuriated the commanders, especially Prien who was sensitive about his new prestige. He learned that three U-boats had attacked the British battleship *Warspite* and all had missed. The aggressive Lemp in U-30 had missed H.M.S. *Barkham,* another battleship, and the *Hood, Nelson,* and *Rodney* had all escaped damage. One report after another told of failure when a glorious victory was within their grasp.

A review of the action showed that U-boats had attacked about twenty-five warships and had sunk only one British submarine. What had gone wrong? Commanders blamed their torpedoes. Was this only an excuse for poor performance? Until now their record of sinkings had been more than acceptable, and previous complaints about torpedoes had been dismissed as alibis. Now, their protests could no longer be ignored without jeopardizing the entire U-boat arm. The incensed Prien told the Obercommando der Marine that he could not be expected to "fight with a dummy rifle." Morale, once high, plummeted as commanders offered weak explanations to their crews.

Doenitz, deeply concerned, demanded an investigation. Experts examined, tested, and reexamined the torpedoes.

Discussions went on for days and weeks. Eventually they discovered that a delicate instrument in the torpedo was at fault because of a change in air pressure. Once the trouble had been remedied, the Norwegian failures were forgotten and the U-boats returned to sinking merchant ships. At least the occupation of Norway gave them a new advantage. Sub bases established on the coast provided much easier access to the Atlantic.

With the fall of France, the U-boat arm gained again. Doenitz built an impregnable base at Lorient on the Bay of Biscay. In September 1940 he moved his headquarters from Wilhelmshaven to Paris and later to Kernevel near Lorient. Other bases built at the French ports of Saint-Nazaire, Brest, La Pallice, and Bordeaux became enormous assets. They saved valuable time and fuel and made it unnecessary for the boats to weave their way through the dangerous inner passages to and from Germany.

In the summer of 1940 the U-boat commanders concentrated on the Western Approaches, the area of the Atlantic near the western ports of Great Britain where the traffic for merchant ships was heaviest. Frequently, U-boats sighted single ships that were easy targets. Convoys increased, but the lack of sufficient escorts made them easy targets, too. Sometimes the U-boats boldly entered between the columns of ships in the convoy, sank one or more of them, and escaped without discovery.

The confidence of the U-boat commanders grew, and they changed their tactics as a result of their experience. Instead of making submerged daytime attacks, they now surfaced at night inside an escort patrol and fired a single torpedo at close range instead of a salvo at long range that only wasted torpedoes.

There were still disappointments, but messages back to base reported a mounting number of successes. Commanders proudly tallied their tonnage sunk: 10,000, then 20,000,

U-251 is welcomed back to its base by a navy band following a successful tour. (PHOTO: U.S. NAVY)

and then 30,000. If they reached 50,000 tons, they were sure of an Iron Cross. No one worried any longer about international law. There were no advance warnings. They did not stop ships to examine papers or check for contraband cargo. The only objective was to attack and sink.

After Norway, Prien could do no wrong. Glorified by the Nazi press, he seemed like a superman. In July he sank 66,588 tons on one patrol. His achievements appeared unlimited as he returned from one cruise after another with new records. One day in August he sank two tankers in quick succession. The second sinking was an accident: a torpedo artificer had lost his balance and fired a torpedo by mistake. Luck was definitely on their side. The next day Prien sank two more tankers.

The second tanker was softened first by gunfire over the objections of Prien's gunner who believed that the sea was too rough for accuracy and that they should not waste their five remaining rounds. Prien insisted and sternly told his gunner, "They must hit." And they did hit.

Kretschmer in U-99 continued to do well, too. On one patrol he returned with seven white pennants flying. He had sunk 65,137 tons and received the Knight's Cross. Grossadmiral Raeder came down to the dock to inspect the crew and was taken aback by the sight of them wearing British uniforms. They had found them in a French warehouse and wore them on patrol as replacements for their soiled outfits. It made no difference. They were the ebullient victors. Two golden horseshoes painted on the conning tower of U-99 seemed to give them extra protection.

Schepke was equally busy. Night operations were still a new technique, but that did not stop him from torpedoing five ships in an outbound convoy in three hours. Schepke, now in command of U-100, had little trouble with the twenty-one ship convoy.

This was the "happy time." Others called it the "golden

age." The delighted Kretschmer said, "We all felt like schoolchildren at Christmas time." The blockade of Britain was working. Soon the Atlantic would be under their sway. Freedom of the seas would become a thing of the past. The Germans would control the seas.

The German people idolized their U-boat aces, and their ranks grew. Endrass, Prien's first watch officer, now had his own boat, and Rollman, Liebe, Frauenheim, and Moehle were names added to the list of aces. These were glorious days for the Third Reich.

From time to time in the fall of 1940, despite the shortage of boats, Doenitz was able to put his *Rudeltaktik* into operation. Doenitz kept in touch with his commanders by radio and relayed to them the news that a convoy was headed for Great Britain. It was SC 7. Determined to attack in numbers, he ordered five boats to form a line across the estimated path of the convoy. The commanders were among his best men.

Five convoy escorts taken by surprise were completely confused by the night action. They had no radar at the time and set off star shells in a futile effort to find the attackers. That only added to the confusion. The U-boats, in their concerted effort, fired their torpedoes and picked off one ship after another. The convoy broke formation in a desperate struggle to escape, making it easier for the U-boats to take on the stragglers. Kretschmer sank them as they lagged behind, and his night's work accounted for six ships. In one night the Allies lost more than 80,000 tons of shipping and almost 100,000 tons of supplies.

The next morning, lookouts on Prien's boat sighted another convoy on its way to a British port. Forty-nine ships made up HX 79; they were loaded with military equipment from the United States. The escort was stronger than usual, but the U-boat commanders saw no reason for that to stop them. Along with Prien, Kretschmer, and Schepke were the aces Bleichrodt and Endrass. HX 79 was in the grip of Germany's all-star team.

The boats remained just beyond the horizon during the day, and when darkness arrived they plunged into the convoy. Through the night, for five long hours, the U-boats sailed up and down the columns of the convoy and caused destruction almost at will. The skies lit up with the flames of doomed ships, and the thunder of an ammunition ship blown to bits was heard for miles. Two tankers burned like torches. It was inconceivable that so few men could create so much damage.

The escorts did their best. They were simply overwhelmed by the coordinated attack. They could not do much more than try to pick up survivors from the cold sea. At that time of year, men could not last long in the water. In five minutes they lost their physical and mental faculties, and in fifteen minutes they were dead. Most of the seamen picked up were badly frostbitten.

When the score was added up for the night, it came to a total of thirteen ships sunk. Prien reported that he had sunk eight ships, and he became the first commander to go over 200,000 tons. Now, he received oak leaves to the Knight's Cross. The triumph on the night of October 19, 1940, could not be exaggerated.

Doenitz continued to be pleased with the statistics that he reviewed. The sinkings far exceeded their small losses. Yet, perhaps needlessly, he had strange forebodings about the future. The aces had done an outstanding job, but he needed still more boats. He had received the go-ahead for new boats, but construction was slower than he had anticipated. Then, too, his boats were almost ridiculously few. Only seven or eight boats operated at one time, and by the end of 1940 he had fewer boats ready for action than he had had at the start of the war. At Christmas he had exactly one boat at sea, an absurd situation. Nevertheless, he had set an outstanding record. This handful of boats had destroyed a battleship, an aircraft carrier, three destroyers, two submarines, five auxiliary cruisers, and more than four hundred merchant ships in the first year of war. He could not deny the record. Still, the nagging worries lingered, and he knew that the slow-moving British would not sit still forever.

4

CONVOYS

Winston Churchill became prime minister of Great Britain in May 1940. He was eligible for an old-age pension. Instead, he led the fight for a free world. The embattled leader faced enemy threats on land, on sea, and in the air. During his early months in office, the British suffered a bitter defeat on the beaches at Dunkirk, the Luftwaffe pounded their ports, and Hitler's plans for Operation Sea Lion, the invasion of Great Britain, were under way. Throughout these terrible days, the only thing that really frightened Churchill, he later said, was the U-boat peril. He admitted that it caused him more anxiety than the famous Battle of Britain that monopolized newspaper headlines throughout the world.

Churchill wrote in his memoirs, "So we poised and pondered the problem." Before long, he set up a new command under Admiral Sir Percy Noble to protect the Western Approaches and strengthen the convoy system. Mainly, this called for more air support, intensive training in antisubmarine tactics, and the construction of new destroyers and other escort ships.

Fortunately, Hitler, after much deliberation, postponed Operation Sea Lion in September. The unenthusiastic

Doenitz feared the consequences of the operation and was probably as relieved as Churchill. The postponement, however, released for escort duty a number of destroyers that the British had held back to protect the homeland. Other aid to Great Britain arrived with the loan of fifty old four-stack destroyers from the United States.

Still, the extra strength was not enough. In the long battle against the U-boat, new detection systems had to be found. Asdic was a help, but it remained insufficient. Churchill supported an all-out effort in research and development. These were bleak days for the British as they fought on alone against the Nazis. Churchill at least gave hope for the future.

Increasingly, the United States, under the sympathetic leadership of President Franklin D. Roosevelt, gave support to Great Britain. In early 1941 Congress passed the Lend-Lease Bill. More money and military supplies were soon on their way to the beleaguered island.

With the cooperation of twenty-one North and South American republics, the Monroe Doctrine once again became a major policy of the Western Hemisphere. These nations agreed on the establishment of a Neutrality Zone that extended 300 to 1,000 miles beyond their shores. These waters, patrolled by the U.S. Navy Atlantic Squadron, were off limits to belligerent warships. This was a clear warning to the Nazis to keep out.

The brilliant Admiral Sir Percy Noble, operating in his own strange and colorful ways, reorganized the antisubmarine forces and stirred them to unprecedented action. Allied ships would no longer be sitting ducks for the U-boats.

Raeder and Doenitz strongly urged Hitler to give them the authority to build more U-boats. So far, U-boat construction had not produced the desired results. More boats were on the way, but not enough. By mid-June 1941 production had improved and about fifteen new boats arrived each month.

In the situation room at Kerneval, Doenitz followed the detailed operations of each boat. Little was overlooked. As more intelligence about allied movements flowed into his headquarters, his control of operations tightened. He personally directed the tactics in the search for convoys. Better informed about the big picture than individual commanders, he ordered boats to specific areas where the possibility of finding a convoy seemed best. This saved time and aimless wandering about the ocean. The critical moment of attack, however, was still left to the judgment of the U-boat commander.

Each morning, at nine sharp, Doenitz met in the situation room with his small staff made up of seasoned U-boat commanders. Each was an expert in a special field such as intelligence, communications, or operations. Like admirals everywhere, Doenitz listened to the latest reports and studied the carefully prepared information on the maps and charts that covered the walls. Pins with flags indicated the position of the boats at sea, and to the best of the Germans' knowledge, they showed the position of Allied ships, also. A diagram posted on the wall gave time zones, tides, currents, ice conditions, fog, and other pertinent facts about the weather. An operation board showed the length of time a boat was at sea, when it was due to return, and the anticipated number of days it would remain in port for repairs or refitting. The room also contained a large globe, more than three feet in diameter, that Doenitz liked to consult for a more realistic image of the world.

In another room called the "museum," graphs showed the number of enemy ships sunk and the U-boat losses. The average sinkings per day at sea and the tonnage totals gave Doenitz a fast summary of the current situation. The exchange rate was never far from his mind.

By now, operations had moved farther west into the Atlantic. One reason for this was that it allowed U-boats to operate beyond the range of British aircraft. So far, aircraft had caused little damage to U-boats, but their searches forced the boats to submerge and made them less effective. Doenitz realized that he needed air support for his submarines. It would be especially helpful in finding the exact location of enemy shipping. U-boats, low to the surface, had poor visibility from the bridge even on the clearest days. Coordinated air and sea reconnaissance and attacks could greatly increase efficiency.

Raeder shared Doenitz's desire for air support. The difficulty was that he received little interest from Reichsmarschall Hermann Goering, the hefty, luxury-loving leader of the Luftwaffe who strongly influenced Hitler and was almost a law unto himself. Goering protested the release of any of his aircraft to support submarines. In his opinion, he had more important things to do elsewhere, and his relations with Raeder had never been very good. Doenitz was disgusted with the excuses that the Luftwaffe gave them for this lack of support. He called them "eagles without wings." By the end of the year, the U-boat arm had received a small concession. Hitler assigned one air group to Doenitz over Goering's objections. It was a miserly contribution, but better than nothing. It certainly did not satisfy Doenitz, who thought it was incomprehensible that he could not have the aircraft he needed to do the job. Air and sea coordination seemed to him so fundamental for modern warfare.

Admiral Sir Percy Noble (and later the equally capable Admiral Sir Max Horton) was just as busy in his situation room at Liverpool. He consulted his maps and charts with the same intensity and tried to counter Doenitz's moves. Each man had professional respect for the other as they played their life and death chess game.

Donald MacIntyre, one of the early escort commanders in the Atlantic, appreciated Sir Percy's grasp of their problems. Escorts aimlessly dashing about the sea in futile chases

A German type VIIIC U-boat returns to its Norwegian port in July 1942. This boat, with 30,000 tons to its credit, is flying the flag of one of its victims. (PHOTO: U.S. NAVY)

produced few results. Organization was the key to success. The only way they could overcome their handicaps was to develop careful teamwork in seeking the enemy. The wild goose chases had to stop.

MacIntyre commanded an old destroyer, *Walker*, as well as an escort group. His job was to give close protection to an Atlantic convoy that might consist of anywhere from forty to eighty ships. When the convoy started its voyage, the escort commander counted and identified each ship. It was hectic work. Then, when the convoy was under way, the problems developed. Ships broke down. Others, lacking speed to keep up with the convoy, straggled behind. A seaman became critically ill and required medical attention. Always anxious, the escort commander practically lived on the bridge in a state of nervous tension.

The escorts—usually about six destroyers, corvettes, and trawlers—formed a circle three to five miles outside the convoy. Each ship was separated from the others by a distance of about eight miles, and each patrolled its section by sailing back and forth, zigzagging most of the time at intervals of about two minutes to confuse the U-boat commanders. MacIntyre said they were like sheep dogs barking at their herd. Communication between ships in the early days was by radio or signal lights.

Most convoy commodores were senior merchant marine officers or admirals who had left the comforts of retirement to battle both the Atlantic and the enemy. Their responsibility, in contrast to that of escort commanders, was to attend to the internal discipline of the convoy, which included navigation and maneuvers. Although they outranked the escort commanders and the differences in their responsibilities were sometimes vague, the commodores were experienced men and usually worked well with the commanders.

The sea itself was an enemy, and good seamanship was basic for survival. The winter of 1940–41 was one of the worst on record, but all winters in the North Atlantic were rough. The escorts rolled and pitched furiously as they carried out their duties, and the danger of collision was always present in the low visibility of stormy days and dark nights. There was no radar until later. Peacetime lights were strictly forbidden, and all ships were totally black.

Normally, U-boat men benefited from poor weather, during which they were not easily sighted, but storms presented dangers, too. The U-boat crews had their own troubles with the North Atlantic winter. The long darkness was depressing, and worse were the frigid temperatures and rough seas that reached hurricane strength. The little boats rolled over on their sides to unbelievable degrees. Men on deck, thrashed by waves, hooked themselves to a stanchion or to the side of the boat. Even so, more than one man was washed overboard by the powerful sea.

Above or below deck, the U-boat men were never warm. After completing a watch on the open bridge, they were almost frozen stiff, and there was no place to warm up. Their clothes were like boards, but they did not take them off because there was no place to thaw them. When they slept in their bunks, they usually wore two or three layers of clothing, which did little good. It was a mystery why pneumonia was not prevalent.

When ice formed on the boat, the vents froze and the ice had to be continually chipped away. Later, special heaters became standard equipment to keep the vents open.

Icebergs were a common hazard. They did, however, provide a good place for U-boats to hide. When the boats were iced over they looked like small icebergs themselves.

When an attack occurred, the problem for the escorts was to find the attacker while protecting the convoy. Sometimes it was almost impossible. The temptation was to leave the convoy and go off on a hunt. The decisions were not easy, and only improved coordination among the escorts

A German lieutenant on his U-boat during a winter patrol in the polar seas off Norway. (PHOTO: U.S. NAVY)

helped solve their dilemmas. Although the increasingly efficient escorts challenged the enemy, their record of effectiveness so far was not impressive.

In March 1941 Günther Prien set out in U-47 for an area south of Iceland. There, in the distance, he sighted a westbound convoy. Prien alerted Joachim Matz in U-70 and Otto Kretschmer in U-99, and the hunt began.

Among the escorts were the destroyers *Wolverine* and *Verity* and the corvettes *Arbutus* and *Camelia*. They commenced depth charging and caught Matz in an awkward position. He dived to 300 feet and remained silent. He knew he was in trouble. His batteries were weak, and he could not stay down too long. The depth charges continued and were so close to the boat that the concussion broke the electric lights. The loss of light increased the fright, but every man knew how to perform his job in the dark. A closer explosion forced the boat out of control to a depth of more than 600 feet. Finally, Matz gained control and reluctantly brought the boat to the surface where he knew the destroyers were waiting for him. They were greeted by gunfire, and the escorts destroyed the U-70, but Matz and most of his crew were saved by the same people who had attacked them.

Shortly after midnight on March 7, Prien began a surface attack from the starboard side of the convoy and was detected. The hydrophone operator on the *Wolverine* reported nearby propeller noises. The captain, Commander James Rowlands, sighted the sub and dashed for it at full speed. Rowlands intended to ram the U-boat, but the canny Prien crash-dived seconds before the destroyer reached him.

Directly overhead, Rowlands dropped a load of depth charges. *Verity* joined the battle, and the two destroyers relentlessly kept up their depth charge attack for five hours. This time asdic was useful as one ship held the contact while the other attacked. Prien made intricate movements to escape, but the destroyers followed him closely.

At 0400 an oil slick appeared on the surface. The U-47 was hurt. At 0424 Prien reported the convoy's position, course, and speed, and then there was silence. At 0519 the U-47 surfaced, and Prien saw the *Wolverine* coming after him. Again, Rowlands intended to ram. Again, Prien crash-dived. But it was all over. In seconds, another round of depth charges erased the asdic contact. The Bull of Scapa Flow was gone.

Kretschmer, in U-99, was nearby. He had heard the depth charges attacking Matz. Forced to dive himself, he now came to the surface and received orders to sink the *Terje Viken,* a huge whaling ship that had been torpedoed and was still afloat. During his unsuccessful search for the ship he heard the base call time and again, "U-47 report your position." The great Prien did not answer.

That night Kretschmer received a message from Lemp

in U-110 that a convoy from Canada was headed eastward off Iceland. Kretschmer, along with Schepke, set out at once for bigger game. The convoy was HX 112, and MacIntyre was the escort commander. Things were not going well for him. Lemp sunk *Erodona*, a 10,000-ton tanker on March 15, and after Kretschmer and Schepke arrived, they torpedoed five ships. The convoy remained together while the escorts laid down a pattern of depth charges that produced no results. At about 0100 on the seventeenth, the destroyer *Vanoc* picked up a clear asdic contact and with the help of *Walker* dropped depth charges that forced a boat to the surface. It was Schepke in U-100. The boat had been badly damaged, and he was trying to make a getaway on the surface.

Vanoc saw the boat and started out at full speed on a course to ram. The cool Schepke thought he could narrowly slip by the destroyer, but he was wrong. The destroyer crashed into the U-boat at a right angle below the conning tower. The hull and conning tower were smashed, and Schepke, on the bridge, was crushed between the caved-in side and the periscope. The *Vanoc* picked up one officer and five enlisted men, but the lively Schepke was not among them. It was then 0300.

The sinking of U-100 made history in another way. The *Vanoc* had a new piece of equipment on board for the detection of submarines. The unit was called "radar" and had not worked too well. This bulky, crude machine with a large antenna reflected radio waves from a solid surface back to a sending set. Eventually, it could pick up targets several miles away. Originally, however, it had not been very useful in finding a small submarine. This eventful night was different. Radar had discovered U-100.

Vanoc signaled to *Walker*, "Have rammed and sunk U-boat." MacIntyre wrote later, "What a blissful moment for us." The joy of the men on the escorts matched the joy of the men in the U-boats after they had sunk a ship. There was no sorrow for the deaths of forty or so of their fellow men. No one talked about humanity. No one asked if war was evil.

Within a half-hour MacIntyre picked up another contact. At first skeptical about the presence of another sub, he decided to attack again. At 0343 he fired six charges. The officer on the bridge of the submarine saw a destroyer coming out of the darkness about a hundred yards away. Startled by the sight of the onrushing ship, he sounded the diving alarm against his standing instructions.

The U-boat commander was below. Now he quickly took over the control of the boat. Once submerged, he believed that his best chance of escaping the depth charges was to maintain an intermediate depth. That night the strategy did not work. The main motors were damaged, water seeped through the pressure hull, and the boat began to sink. The commander ordered all tanks blown with the intention of rising to just below the surface. Instead, the damaged boat broke the surface.

As the *Walker* turned to make another attack, the *Vanoc* signaled that a submarine was coming to the surface. It was the U-99. The *Vanoc* spotted the boat in its searchlight beam and commenced firing. Then the *Walker* started firing.

Kretschmer, on the bridge of U-99, ordered the crew on deck where they tried to find protection behind the conning tower. The engineer reported that the boat was unable to submerge. The only alternative was to abandon ship. Kretschmer ordered the destruction of secret documents while gunfire ripped across the sea.

A signal from the boat in broken English flashed through the darkness. It said, "We are sunking." The firing ceased, and MacIntyre cautiously prepared to lower a lifeboat. Men were already in the water as the U-boat slowly sank.

Kretschmer realized that there was a possibility that the

boat might be captured before it went down. He told the engineer to vent aft by loosening the valves a fraction on their seatings. But the air rushed out, and bow went up, and then the boat sank with the engineer still inside. Kretschmer was standing by the conning tower hatch ready to give the engineer a hand up. In an instant, he was washed into the sea with the rest of his men.

MacIntyre, a skillful seaman, maneuvered his ship to windward and then drifted toward the survivors. The men they fished out of the ocean were near exhaustion. Some could thank the courage of Leading Seaman Prout who dived into the water to help them. MacIntyre said that one man was almost given up as dead. He appeared stone cold, but someone suggested that they might defrost him in the warm galley. It worked, and the man came back to life.

Later, when MacIntyre became acquainted with Kretschmer, he was surprised to find such a quiet, unwarlike man who did not seem to be an ardent Nazi. Kretschmer had once studied at Exeter University in England and spoke good English. Since the ship was small, the prisoner had considerable freedom on board and even played bridge in the wardroom with some of the British officers. Once again, men face to face treated one another in a humane, civilized manner. Yet, a short time before, these same men had been deadly enemies who were committed to kill one another. It was a strange world.

One day, on the quarterdeck, Kretschmer noticed that the ship's insignia was a horseshoe. He mentioned to one of the ship's chief petty officers that his boat had also displayed horseshoes. There was, however, a difference. Kretschmer said that his horseshoes pointed down while the British horseshoes pointed up. The chief replied that the British believed that horseshoes pointed down only let all the luck run out. Kretschmer, without saying a word, seemed to agree. His luck had certainly run out. All his torpedoes had been used before he had been discovered, and he had simply been trying to return home safely. At any rate, he was still luckier than his fellow aces Prien and Schepke. Kretschmer had also done more than his share of damage. He had sunk 325,000 tons, more than any other German ace. American submarines operating in the Pacific would never attain such a figure. Their highest record was 100,000 tons.

In a few brief days Doenitz had lost three of his top aces. The blow was crushing and, as always, he looked for a cause. What had gone wrong? From the bits of information that he received, he concluded that no one could be blamed for the tragic series of events.

That same spring Lemp in U-110, the commander who had torpedoed the *Athenia* on the first day of the war, sighted a convoy and reported to headquarters. Adalbert Schnee, commander of U-201, intercepted the message and realized that he could rendezvous with Lemp. Early on the morning of May 9 the boats came close enough for the two men to shout back and forth. After a brief conference, they decided to make a submerged daylight attack after maneuvering into proper position. Schnee was to follow Lemp's initial attack in a half-hour.

By noon Lemp had fired torpedoes that hit two ships. He was off to a good start when an alert escort, H.M.S. *Aubretia*, sighted Lemp's periscope. Two other escorts, H.M.S. *Broadway* and H.M.S. *Bulldog*, joined in dropping depth charges in the vicinity. About thirty minutes later their ferocious attack forced Lemp to the surface.

Captain Baker-Cresswell on the *Bulldog* started to ram the submarine and then changed his mind. Thinking that he might capture the helpless U-110, he altered his course. The crew of the U-boat, desperate to escape, streamed out of the conning tower hatch and jumped into the sea. Lemp was last seen in the water with his men, asking about various crew members. Then he disappeared.

Sublieutenant David Balme of the *Bulldog* led a small

boarding party in a whaler. They rowed to the U-110, found it deserted, and proceeded to remove everything possible that might have intelligence value. Everyone on the *Bulldog* was ignorant about operating a submarine so they took it in tow with the hope of reaching Iceland. Unfortunately, the boat sank the next day while en route.

In August Squadron Leader J. H. Thompson, flying a Hudson from Iceland, sighted the U-570 on the surface. He attacked with depth charges and several straddled the boat. To his surprise, he saw a white flag waving on the conning tower. Thompson reported his conquest to his base, but there was no ship in the area to come to his immediate aid. Instead, Flying Officer E. A. Jewiss, a Catalina pilot, joined him, and they circled the boat as long as their fuel lasted. Twelve hours later, the trawler *Northern Chief* appeared on the scene and found that the hapless commander, Hans Rahmlow, could not dive or even scuttle the boat for some reason. The next day, the trawler towed the boat in a rough sea to Iceland where it was beached. Later the boat sailed to England where it was converted to H.M.S. *Graph.*

Rahmlow's crew was taken to the camp in which Kretschmer was a prisoner. Secretly and illegally, some of the prisoners conducted a court of honor and decided that all the crew of the U-570 were innocent except the first watch officer. In their opinion, he should have arrested Rahmlow or scuttled the boat.

Later, the prisoners learned that H.M.S. *Graph* was anchored nearby at Barrow-in-Furness. The guilty first watch officer was informed by his fellow prisoners that he might redeem himself if he sank the boat. The poor man, suffering with his name under a cloud, accepted the challenge and was shot during the attempt.

Rahmlow arrived at the camp after the judgment had been handed down on his first watch officer. He was treated as an outcast, and when the British authorities learned of the awkward situation he was moved to another camp.

During this summer Doenitz moved his boats back to the North Channel for a while, but by September he had more boats available and sent them out into the Atlantic again. The British had improved their methods, but the U-boat arm was now stronger than ever, and the greatest convoy battles were still ahead.

Despite setbacks, Doenitz contented himself with the thought that his group tactics were working. In the early days of the war, while having dinner with some naval officers on a train traveling from Wilhelmshaven to Berlin, Doenitz talked about the value of catchphrases. Then he wrote on a napkin, *"U-boote sind die Wolfe zur See: angreifen, reissen, versenken!"* ("U-boats are the wolves of the sea: attack, tear, sink!") The idea took hold, and German submariners liked to think of themselves as sea wolves. Now, as the boats operated in groups, they were referred to as wolf packs.

When a boat commander sighted a convoy, he reported his find to headquarters and trailed the target. Meanwhile, Doenitz radioed other boats in the vicinity, giving the convoy position, course, and speed. Then as many boats as possible, at full speed on the surface, flocked together for the attack. Sometimes the first boat guided the others to their rendezvous with the help of homing signals.

A half-dozen or more U-boats might attack the convoy from each side and create utter confusion. The still weak escorts were often outnumbered and could do little to prevent chaos. By September 1941 Doenitz was able to set up scouting patrols of ten, fifteen, or twenty submarines. More would be heard from the wolf packs.

5

UNDECLARED WAR

In June 1941 Kapitänleutnant Rolf Mützelburg, commander of U-203, sighted the battleship U.S.S. *Texas* and a screen of destroyers just before dusk. They were steaming off Greenland, ten miles inside the war zone where Germans had declared that all shipping might be sunk on sight. Mützelburg radioed a sighting report to headquarters and then immediately chased the American ships in an effort to attack. A sharp-eyed American lookout, however, saw a periscope less than a 1,000 yards off the port quarter, and the *Texas* altered course. Mützelburg followed for 140 miles until rough seas and the zigzagging of his target made the pursuit futile. Nonetheless, he was luckier than he thought.

The next day Mützelburg received a message that read, "By order of the fuehrer: All incidents with the United States must be avoided in the coming weeks. Until further notice, attacks may not be made on battleships, cruisers, and aircraft carriers unless positively identified as hostile."

Mützelburg had had a close call. He had narrowly avoided creating a grave international incident. Hitler had his reasons for the restraining order, but he kept them a dark secret.

The activities of the U.S. Navy were becoming an

increasing nuisance to Doenitz. There was no doubt that Americans escorted British ships to Iceland, shadowed U-boats, and reported their positions to the British. No one could question the importance of this aid to the Allies. Doenitz wanted to act and asked for permission to attack American shipping. He advised Hitler that Germany's meek acceptance of American interference would render their blockade of England useless.

As early as April the United States destroyer *Niblack* had rushed to the rescue of the sinking *Saleir*, a Dutch freighter. While picking up survivors, a lookout sighted a submarine, and the destroyer dropped three depth charges. The submarine escaped, but the incident was undoubtedly reported to Hitler.

Although the North Atlantic was the major scene of U-boat activity, the *Robin Moor*, an American freighter, was torpedoed in the South Atlantic. The incidents with the Americans started to pile up.

Hitler knew that submarine attacks had been the main cause for America's entry into World War I, and he wanted to avoid making the same mistake. These were sensitive days, and he had no wish to antagonize the United States unnecessarily.

By June 22 Hitler's reasons for avoiding war with the United States became obvious. That day 120 German divisions invaded the Soviet Union, the beginning of Operation Barbarossa.

The fuehrer wrote to Doenitz on July 25, 1941, "I want to avoid, however, a declaration of war by the United States while the eastern campaign is still in progress, especially as the army is still involved in heavy fighting. But I will never call a submarine commander to account if he torpedoes an American ship by mistake. After the eastern campaign I reserve the right to take severe action against the U.S.A. as well."

About the same time that Hitler wrote to Doenitz, President Roosevelt sent American troops to Iceland to serve as a bulwark of defense. He did not want Nazi Germany to dominate the Atlantic and destroy the freedom of the seas.

The following month, President Roosevelt let it be known that he intended to leave his desk at the White House for a few days and go on a fishing trip. Everyone agreed that a little relaxation would do him good. He gathered some friends together and boarded the presidential yacht *Potomac* at New London, Connecticut.

The President spent the next day around Buzzards Bay off Massachusetts. The fishing was not too good, but Franklin Roosevelt always enjoyed the sea, and he appeared to be having a grand vacation. That evening, he drove a speedboat to a nearby yacht club and dropped off some of his guests who had been on the yacht. Among them were Princess Martha of Norway and Prince Karl of Sweden.

The next day, the *Potomac* sailed through the Cape Cod canal in full view of hundreds of vacationers. Many of the sightseers watching the beautiful yacht undoubtedly deceived themselves into believing that they saw the President on the deck, but he was not on board. He had slipped away and boarded the cruiser U.S.S. *Augusta* off Martha's Vineyard.

The President and his military chiefs on the *Augusta* sailed to a secret rendezvous in Argentia Bay, Newfoundland, where H.M.S. *Prince of Wales* appeared. On board the British ship was Prime Minister Winston Churchill.

The two leaders were keenly aware that this was a historic event. Each man had an opportunity to size up the other as they talked over light and serious matters. There was no doubt that the prime minister wanted the United States to declare war. The wary President merely showed his friendship while remaining aloof from any final declarations.

Nevertheless, the dramatic and significant meeting

strengthened the Anglo-American relationship and produced a mutual statement called the Atlantic Charter. When the two leaders reached home, the news was released to the world that the two great nations of the free world stood together.

The next month there was another tense incident at sea. The U.S.S. *Greer*, a destroyer, was on a mail run to Iceland in waters that the Germans considered a war zone and that the Americans regarded as a defense zone. A British plane signaled the destroyer that a submerged U-boat lurked in its way. The ship zigzagged and picked up the boat on its sonar, the American name for asdic. The destroyer reported the exact position of the submarine to the British.

About an hour later, the plane dropped four depth charges in the area of the contact and then, short of fuel, returned to base. The submarine was not hit, and the destroyer trailed it. After about two hours, the submarine fired torpedoes at the *Greer*. The destroyer evaded the attack and then dropped depth charges. During this action, the *Greer* lost contact, then picked it up again and dropped more depth charges without effect. Finally, the *Greer* discontinued its chase and left the British to carry on.

In a fireside chat, President Roosevelt reported the episode to the American people. He declared, "This was piracy, piracy legally and morally. . . . We have no shooting war with Hitler. We do not seek it now. But . . . when you see a rattlesnake poised to strike, you do not wait until he has struck before you crush him."

Roosevelt ordered the navy to shoot on sight. The commander of the Atlantic fleet received authority to protect American convoys to Iceland and the ships of any nation that joined these convoys. Supporting these orders, Secretary of the Navy Frank Knox said, "The navy is ordered to capture or destroy by every means at its disposal Axis-controlled submarines or surface raiders in these waters. That is our answer to Mr. Hitler."

In October one or more U-boats south of Iceland located a slow convoy of forty ships with only four corvettes for escort. The Nazis had a field day. When the first three ships were sunk, the convoy escorts asked the base at Iceland for help. Five American destroyers sped to the area at once, but they had no radar, and the submarines were out of range of their sound gear. The Germans, undisturbed by the depth charges that the destroyers aimlessly dropped, sank seven more ships.

One American destroyer, the U.S.S. *Kearney*, stopped to permit a corvette to cross its bow. This unfortunate lapse gave a U-boat sufficient time to fire a torpedo, which damaged the destroyer and killed eleven seamen. Although the ship returned to Iceland, American blood had been spilled on a warship.

President Roosevelt angrily said, "We have wished to avoid shooting. But the shooting has started. And history has recorded who has fired the first shot. In the long run, however, all that will matter is who fired the last shot."

Worse was still to come. At the end of October, 600 miles off Ireland, outside American waters, a U-boat sank the destroyer U.S.S. *Reuben James*. Only forty-five of the crew survived. Still, war was not declared, and the strain told on both sides. The lack of a clear-cut situation was a handicap for commanders, friend or foe, who could never be completely sure of their authority to act.

Although war with America was inevitable, the next move came as a surprise to Hitler. He had not known anything about the Japanese plans to attack Pearl Harbor. December 7, 1941, the "Day of Infamy," changed everything. Open hostilities between the United States and the Axis powers were now a foregone conclusion. On December 8 the U.S. Congress declared war on Japan, and three days later, Germany and Italy declared war on the United States.

The restless Doenitz, anxious to attack American ships, now had his wish. He wasted no time recalling boats from

The crew at work on U-94 in 1941. (PHOTO: BUNDESARCHIV)

far-off stations in the Atlantic and the Mediterranean to prepare for an onslaught off the American coast. He remembered that his U-boats had produced remarkable results off the harbors of the British Isles while the enemy was unprepared. Now, he hoped to repeat the performance off the east coast of the United States.

Late in December Doenitz sent the first few boats across the Atlantic to take stations off the American coast. He selected some of his best commanders. Among them were Reinhard Hardegen, Ernst Kals, and Heinrich Bleichrodt. This time each commander would operate alone.

The long voyage across the Atlantic took time and fuel.

Only successful sinkings would make the expedition worthwhile. Although a larger Type IX boat had been built, the only boats available for the operation were the Type VII workhorses with their limited range.

U-boat crews were so eager to tackle the Americans that they were ready to make almost any sacrifice. The cramped quarters became more cramped as they took on extra stores for the long cruise. There was hardly room to move. Piled on each side of the narrow passageway were crates of supplies, and some crews went so far as to fill water tanks with extra fuel. No one wanted to miss the excitement.

6

THE AMERICAN COAST

Hardegen, following orders from headquarters, took his station off Cape Hatteras, North Carolina. He was not to prowl around looking for targets. Instead, his orders were to wait and see what came his way. He had already received the code word to attack, *Paukenschlag*, which means "bang the kettledrum," and he did not have long to wait.

Early on the morning of January 18, 1942, Hardegen spotted a heavily loaded tanker. The *Allan Jackson* was a Standard Oil of New Jersey ship carrying thousands of barrels of Colombian crude oil. The time was 0130, the night was clear, and the outline of the ship made a highly visible target. Hardegen went to work. Two torpedoes ripped into the ship, split the bow, and started a fire. Two seamen on the forecastle of the tanker were immediately killed, and the second mate and another seaman on the bridge were blown into the sea.

The captain of the *Allan Jackson*, ironically named Felix Kretchmer, was in his cabin at the time of the explosion. He was thrown out of his bunk, and as he struggled to find his way to the bridge the fire raced through the ship. He heard excruciating shrieks from some of his men burning alive, and the ship was already sinking as he tried to climb a ladder. Before he reached the bridge, he was swept overboard and sucked under the sea.

In the midst of disaster, Kretchmer was lucky. He came to the surface beyond the flaming waters and found a plank to grasp. While fighting to remain afloat, he had a good look at the awesome U-boat. As he watched the harrowing sight, he could do nothing except hope that help would soon arrive. Seven long hours passed, and then miraculously a destroyer found him.

Some of the crew had managed to launch a lifeboat and fought clear of the spinning propeller of the tanker. But when the casualties were counted, twenty-two men were lost in the first sinking of an American ship in the newly declared war.

Hardegen had made a good start. In the next few days other sinkings by U-boats followed off the coast with unbelievable ease. The *City of Atlanta, Frances Salman, Norvana,* and *Venore* were lost within the week, and others soon joined the growing list.

On February 2 another Standard Oil of New Jersey tanker, *W. L. Steed,* sailing northeasterly, bucked a northwest wind of gale proportions and a heavy snowstorm off the Delaware Capes. The struggle against the rough weather was enough for any seaman, but at 1245 a torpedo struck the ship on the starboard side. Again, oil caught fire and blazed through the ship.

The captain ordered the second mate to ready lifeboats for lowering. Despite the heavy seas and the raging fire, the boats were safely launched. The entire crew seemed to have escaped, and yet their troubles had only begun.

Fourteen men in one lifeboat watched not one, but two gray U-boats shell the *Steed* until it went down. Then the frigid temperature took its toll among the men huddled in the lifeboat. Within three days, twelve men had died. On the fourth day, a steamship passed by. The hopes of the two remaining survivors were dashed when there was no recognition from the ship. Then, as all seemed lost, the ship turned around and picked up the two men. The rescue ship was a British freighter, *Hartlepool*, bound for Halifax. When they reached their destination the two men were taken to a hospital. Unfortunately, only one recovered.

Meanwhile, another lifeboat was on the verge of swamping. The men bailed frantically for a couple of hours and then crouched under the canvas boat cover in an attempt to keep warm. The experience was simply too much for one young seaman who went to sleep and did not wake up. Another man became delirious and soon died.

In desperation, the men poured oil from a lamp onto some wood in a water bucket and started a fire. Able Seaman Ralph Mazzucco thought it saved their lives. They kept it burning by cutting up sails, the bottom board, and one of the oars. It lasted about a day, which was sufficient because the three survivors were saved by a Canadian auxiliary cruiser, H.M.C.S. *Alcantara*.

A third boat from the *Steed* with four men was found 400 miles out to sea by the British *Raby Castle* on February 12. It was too late. Three men had already died, and the fourth lingered only three days after the rescue. In all, thirty-four men had made up the crew of the *Steed*, and only four survived.

Such stories were repeated time and again as the U-boats boldly carried their war within sight of the American shore. Few of the stories appeared in the press, but sometimes people watched the action from the beaches of New Jersey or Florida. On rare occasions, pilots and passengers in commercial planes flying down the coast saw daylight submarine attacks. And the grimmest reminders were the bodies of American seamen that washed up on the beaches.

Later in February, William Briden, a police sergeant in

Belmar, New Jersey, saw flames shoot high into the sky. He could hardly believe his eyes. How could a U-boat dare to attack a ship so close to the American shore? The ship was the *R. P. Resor*, another tanker headed north, and it was torpedoed from inshore. At about 2300, Able Seaman John Forsdal relieved the lookout on the forecastle. They were then about twenty miles east of Manasquan Inlet. Forsdal saw something dark off the port bow and thought it was a fishing boat. Since they were so close to shore there was little likelihood of a submarine. Then he saw navigational lights only 200 yards away.

Forsdal struck the bell twice and reported to the bridge, "Small vessel about two points on your port bow." In seconds a torpedo exploded on the port side, and the impact knocked Forsdal down. When he got up he saw the submarine, which appeared to be headed for the shore and then vanished. By now the tanker was a roaring fire, and Forsdal went over the side by going down a line that was hanging alongside. The water around the ship was thick with heavy oil, but not yet on fire. He swam awkwardly out to sea until he heard the voice of the radio operator. Exhausted, they both climbed onto a raft floating nearby.

Since the action was so clearly seen from the shore, boats set out at once to help. Despite the quick rescue efforts, there was little success. A Coast Guard boat found the two men on the raft, but the radio operator was dead. One other man was picked up in the sea for a total of two survivors.

A Coast Guardsman said that the oil on Forsdal had congealed, and they had to cut off his clothes and life jacket. "Even his mouth," he said, "was filled with a blob of oil."

During the same month, U-128 and U-504 found easy targets off the Florida coast. U-504 sank the tanker *Republic* within sight of Jupiter Inlet. In about an hour two lifeboats reached shore with some of the crew.

U-96 coming into Saint-Nazaire in 1941. (PHOTO: BUNDESARCHIV)

The ship went down in only six fathoms of water. The stern rested on the bottom, and the bow stuck up in the air. Two adventurous young men took their boat out in daylight for a closer look and discovered a lonely wirehaired fox terrier on board. They took the dog off the ship and returned happily to shore.

Although the American people knew about the submarine menace, they were not aware of the extent of the threat. Near the end of February, Secretary of the Navy Knox reported to the press that three U-boats had been sunk and four probably damaged. This was an optimistic claim that he may have believed at the time. Observers were never too accurate in telling what they saw. Actually, the U-boats remained off the coast unharmed by any American antisubmarine efforts.

The war had begun in Europe two years before, but the United States was still unprepared for antisubmarine warfare. Before Pearl Harbor both the chief of naval operations and the commander of the Atlantic Fleet had requested funds for meeting a submarine threat and were turned down.

Now, Admiral Adolphus Andrews, commander of the Eastern Sea Frontier, tried to cope with a situation that approached disastrous dimensions. The bad news that he received at his headquarters on Church Street in New York City was endless. He battled the U-boats with resources that were far too slender.

Step by step Andrews tackled the problem. He saw to it that mines were laid off the major harbors on the East Coast, that ships were routed to inland waterways as much as possible, and that the Army Air Force sent three planes each from its bases at Westover Field, Massachusetts; Mitchell Field, Long Island; and Langley Field, Virginia. Yet these efforts were pathetically meager and produced few positive results.

About two months after America's entry into the war, 145 ships had been sunk and 600 men lost. During March 1942 the devastation mounted as the losses for that one month matched the total for January and February. Two ships were actually shelled within view of sightseers on the Atlantic City boardwalk.

The American Merchant Marine Institute estimated that the average ship carried a cargo that would fill four trains of seventy-five cars each. A standard tanker of the time, it was said, transported enough gasoline to furnish a motorist with a wartime A-ration book enough fuel for 35,000 years.

The tanker losses were undoubtedly the most critical.

The war could not be won without gasoline in the right place at the right time. The coastal route was vital because petroleum was shipped north from the oil fields of Texas and Venezuela. If the tanker losses continued at the same rate as they had during the first two months, the armed forces would not have enough fuel to fight the war.

The surprising element in this threatening situation was that Doenitz had caused this destruction with so few boats. Hardegen alone sank eight ships amounting to 53,360 tons on his first patrol off the American coast. There were never more than twelve U-boats along the coast at one time. About half of the twenty-two boats at sea were on their way to or from base.

At the end of March, the *City of New York* had safely crossed the Atlantic from Cape Town only to be sunk off Hatteras Inlet. In the midst of the horror that cost the lives of many passengers and crew, one woman gave birth to a baby girl. The U.S.S. *Jesse Roper* came to the rescue, and the new mother named her baby Jesse Roper Noharovic.

Slowly, Andrews built the Eastern Sea Frontier into a stronger organization. He received little help when he requested escort ships from the chief of naval operations because warships were needed in the Pacific and for transatlantic convoys. There were just not enough to go around. Coastal shipping remained a neglected child. Nevertheless, some help arrived. Two blimps became a part of the antisubmarine defense, and others soon joined them. Although they were little use for engaging in battle against a submarine, they were helpful for observation. One blimp dared to attack, but the submarine gun crew easily punctured the slow-moving blimp's gasbag and forced it into the water with the loss of one man.

A few more aircraft, some seventy- and eighty-foot Coast Guard boats, and a number of private yachts and sailboats also joined the Eastern Sea Frontier. Some of the very rich had turned over their magnificent yachts to the United States Maritime Commission. Among the donors were Henry Ford and Joseph Davies, former ambassador to the Soviet Union. William Vanderbilt gave up his handsome three-million-dollar *Alva* for the duration of the war.

Sailboats were used as picket boats and had one advantage. They were noiseless and so could not be detected by submarine sound gear. Like blimps, they were no match for a submarine in a fight and were useful only to make possible sightings.

Andrews found that one simple precaution against U-boats was difficult to enforce. He learned that three ships were lost in the first month because they were clearly shown up against the lights on shore. A blackout was ordered along the coast, but many selfish local merchants resisted because they felt it hurt their business.

By April Andrews had begun the first coastal convoys. They departed from the Florida strait for Charleston where they spent the night and then moved north to the Chesapeake, New York, and through the Cape Cod Canal where they eventually met British and Canadian escorts. At Halifax, some coastal ships joined Atlantic convoys.

Many old-time merchant marine captains were not happy about joining slow convoys or following routes prescribed by the U.S. Navy. They preferred to place confidence in their own judgment. One of their fears was the danger of going aground while hugging the coastline. They were not always right, and only time and wartime experience improved the working relationship between the navy and the merchant marine.

America's lack of preparedness was a big advantage for the U-boats. In the first three months of war, as they torpedoed one ship after another, not a single U-boat was damaged. The "second happy time" had begun, and enthusiasm among the U-boat men soared.

U-123 in the Atlantic. (PHOTO: BUNDESARCHIV-MILITARCHIV)

Kapitänleutnant Eberhard Greger, in U-85, operating off Chesapeake Bay, came up for air one night in mid-April. He had found little to fear from defense patrols. Nearby, however, the destroyer *Roper*, using its new radar equipment, spotted the submarine. The captain, Lieutenant Commander H. W. Howe, sounded general quarters, increased his speed, and closed in on the boat.

Greger fired a torpedo, but the destroyer turned hard to starboard and he missed his target. Then Howe switched on his big searchlight and had a good look at U-85. Greger, trying to get out of the glare of the beam, maneuvered sharply. Howe stayed on his trail. In the middle of the night the two captains fought a deadly duel.

Greger ordered his gun crew on deck, and the *Roper*'s machine guns mowed the Germans down as they appeared. Other U-boat men came up on deck as the destroyer guns hit the boat and it started sinking. Howe was ready to fire a torpedo when the boat disappeared.

In these few minutes of action the lucky streak of the U-boat ran out. Submarine men abandoned the boat and swam around in the oily water, some wearing escape lungs. Howe persisted in the attack. Too many American ships had been lost, and too many ineffectual months had gone by to expect him to show softness toward the enemy. The American mood impatiently insisted on destroying this scourge of the sea.

The destroyer captain was determined to make certain of his kill. A "possible" or "probable" kill was not enough for him, and he made no effort to pick up survivors. Instead, he dropped eleven depth charges in the area where he last saw the sub, and the concussion killed all the men in the water. Howe, still making sure, remained in the vicinity until daylight. Two patrol planes joined him, and other ships picked up twenty-nine bodies in the water. After four months of war, this was the first American sinking of a U-boat.

Although Doenitz never liked a loss, he could not help being pleased when he looked at the exchange rate. By the end of April, his records showed that he had sunk 198 ships and lost only one submarine. He did not expect the second happy time to last, but he intended to make the most of it as long as possible.

In a report to Hitler, Doenitz admitted that American defenses would certainly improve. At the time, however, he told the fuehrer that a number of American deficiencies were a boon for the U-boat men. As he analyzed the situation, the American air defense was one serious weakness. The few inexperienced pilots saw nothing. And, on the sea, the antisubmarine patrols moved too fast to detect underwater vessels. He also claimed that the Americans did not pursue the enemy with perseverance.

Doenitz, like everyone, enjoyed reporting good news. Nevertheless, he used the opportunity to warn Hitler that eventually the Americans would be better organized and that German losses would rise again. He knew that the Americans could mine the coast, set up antisubmarine nets, and make coastal convoys more effective. Germans must strive to improve U-boat weapons. He said, "The most important thing in this respect is the development of the torpedo with the noncontact pistol." His eye was on the future.

By May U-boat commanders off the American coast

noticed that it was not quite so easy to pick off ships. The Americans had learned from experience, and their methods were now more efficient. Helmut Rathke, commanding U-352, found this to be true, and he was disappointed that he did not find more targets.

On May 9 Rathke saw a warship approaching. It was the Coast Guard Cutter *Icarus*, whose men had heard the submarine on their sound gear. Rathke fired a torpedo, but to his dismay it exploded before reaching the target.

Icarus increased speed and laid down a pattern of depth charges. Nothing seemed to happen. They dropped more depth charges, and then the U-boat broke the surface. Gun crews on the cutter commenced firing, and one shell ricocheted and tore through the conning tower, taking one man's arm and another man's leg.

In a few minutes Rathke ordered the men to abandon ship. Many men escaped as the U-352 went down. Lieutenant Commander Maurice Jester, captain of the *Icarus*, did not stop the fight to pick up survivors. Now, like Howe, he dropped depth charges, but apparently they were too far off to harm the swimmers. Rathke swam around trying to rally his men. He tied a tourniquet on the man who had lost his leg and told his men not to talk if they were captured.

Icarus circled the survivors without picking them up. After a lapse of a number of minutes, the cutter received a message from the Seventh Naval District to rescue survivors. The purpose was to gain intelligence rather than to save lives. Those fished out of the sea were taken to Charleston where the wounded were treated. The man who had lost his arm was in such severe pain that he begged in English for someone to shoot him. The man who lost his leg soon died. Intelligence officers questioned the others, who followed Rathke's orders and did not talk.

Although the Americans could claim another sub sinking, they were a long way from gaining the upper hand. Their losses continued, and the situation remained critical.

One loss about this time was the converted 250-foot yacht *Cythera*, which left Norfolk for Pearl Harbor. The *Cythera* did not get very far. Off Cape Fear, North Carolina, a torpedo crashed into the ship, and only two men of a crew of seventy survived the explosion. Baron Siegfried Freiher von Forstner, the U-boat commander, saw the two men gasping in the water and against strict orders from Doenitz took pity on them and brought them aboard.

Things had not been going too well for the thirty-two-year-old Prussian aristocrat who commanded U-402. A professional naval officer from a family of military men, von Forstner had served on the pocket battleship *Admiral Scheer* and the cruiser *Nürnberg*, but the duty did not completely satisfy his daring, aggressive spirit. When war broke out, he transferred to the U-boat service in the hope that he would see more action. He was fortunate to receive some of his training from Silent Otto Kretschmer, but his early U-boat career was disappointing.

For five months von Forstner's appetite for action was not fulfilled because he was assigned as commander of a training boat. Then he received command of U-402. Even then his first three patrols were not very successful. He had sunk only one ship, near the Azores, and was disgusted with his record. Although his latest sinking helped, he was now on his way back to Saint-Nazaire since he had no more torpedoes.

The baron, a correct Prussian, was neither a fervent Nazi nor a man who held personal grudges against the enemy. He found his captives "nice chaps" who were friendly and relieved to be alive. Destiny seemed to be at work in the lives of his prisoners. Some men lived against all odds. One of the Americans had been a member of the crew of the ill-fated *Oklahoma* at Pearl Harbor and could still tell the tale. In this early stage of the war he had seen more action than most men experience in their entire lives.

Baron von Forstner, commander of U-402, at Saint-Nazaire in 1942. (PHOTO: BUNDESARCHIV)

Von Forstner knew that he should lock up his prisoners, but there was really no space, and he saw no risk in giving them the limited freedom of the boat. At mealtime the prisoners ate with the crew, and everyone got along well without hatred or bitterness.

The baron wrote to his young wife, the Baroness Annamaria von Forstner, that when they arrived at Saint-Nazaire the Americans in his custody "were met by an escort and taken away in the usual manner thought fit for prisoners of war, much to the consternation of my crew, whom they had invited to come and see them back home in the States after the war."

The distance from the sub bases on the French coast to the area of operation remained one of the major problems for the U-boat arm. The Type VII U-boat lacked fuel capacity for a long cruise and had to be refueled. At first, surface vessels were used for this purpose until one by one the Allies sank them. Clearly, another answer had to be found for the supply question.

The answer to the supply question soon became obvious to the German strategists. If surface ships failed, submarines should supply submarines. Doenitz gave orders for building a submarine tanker. The first was U-459. It carried 700 tons of fuel and no weapons. This ingenious idea allowed U-boats to increase their operating periods. Officially, the supply boats were called Type XIV; unofficially they became popularly known as *milch cows* (milk cows). They were also useful for delivering fresh food and taking off sick or wounded seamen.

Another disadvantage for U-boat commanders was the continual need to surface to recharge the huge 100-ton batteries that powered the electric motors under the sea. The diesels had to turn over the electric motors to reenergize the batteries, and this could not be done without air to breathe. The process took two or three hours and exposed the boats to attack, especially from aircraft.

At the time most U-boat commanders believed that, at worst, aircraft were merely a nuisance. Although they forced the boats to submerge, they generally saw little, and their attacks were far wide of the mark. Nevertheless, there were exceptions.

During the summer Horst Degen, commander of U-701, had spent a long time on the bottom off Cape Hatteras. He had to come up for air before everyone suffocated, and he needed to recharge the vessel's batteries. It was midafternoon. It would have been better to wait until night, but that was not possible. Besides, recharging a battery at night had its own dangers. Lookouts could not see the enemy, and the noise of the diesels drowned out the sound of approaching aircraft.

Degen saw nothing through his periscope, and so he surfaced. The fresh air was a tremendous relief for everyone, and the commander and lookouts saw nothing to worry about.

At the same time, however, Second Lieutenant Harry Kane, pilot of a Lockheed-Hudson, was making a routine patrol. He had a boring time. Day after day he took off from his shore base, droned on and on for hours, and saw nothing to report. This day was different.

Kane's altitude was only 1,000 feet when to his amazement he saw a submarine. He was also lucky. The sun was at his back, and the lookouts could not see his plane. He started a bombing run, and as he closed in on the boat, the lookouts finally saw the plane.

Degen crash-dived. Since aircraft were notoriously inaccurate, Degen had little reason to believe that he would not be safe under the sea. It was one more close call, he thought.

Kane dropped his first depth charge, but it fell short. The second and third damaged the hull, however, and the boat surfaced. Degen ordered his men to abandon ship, and in the commotion he fell, hit his head, and lost consciousness. By now, water rushed into the boat as the men scrambled around in depths up to their waists.

Kane watched the hectic activity below as he circled and circled. He counted seventeen men in the water and showed concern for them. He dropped four life rafts and a lifeboat and sent out a message for help for the men in the water. A Panamanian freighter received the message but feared stopping for a rescue effort and continued on its way.

A Coast Guard cutter also received a message from Kane, but the location of the sinking was mixed up in transmission so they gave no assistance. By then the victorious Kane had to return to base before he ran out of fuel.

Meanwhile, the Germans tried to remain afloat. The rafts that Kane had dropped were too far in the distance, so they were left to their own devices. The men had dragged the unconscious commander with them, and he was an extra burden because he had no life jacket. The men, growing weaker all the time, took turns holding him above the water.

Hours turned into days without help in sight. The engineering officer lost his mind, let out horrible screams, and drowned. Three men decided to swim to shore, and they were never seen again. Seven men remained together, and by the end of the second day they had drifted 60 miles in the Gulf Stream.

When the end became almost inevitable, the bulky blimp K-8 appeared. Hovering above, men in the ungainly airship lowered a raft, blankets, and medical equipment. By afternoon, a Coast Guard seaplane, responding to the blimp's message, landed in the water and flew the survivors to Norfolk.

As the coastal convoys increased off the eastern United States, Doenitz moved a number of his boats south into the Caribbean. Again the Germans found easy and valuable targets, many of them tankers.

The U-505, operating in the Caribbean, came across the liberty ship, *Thomas McKean*, torpedoed it, and then surfaced. Still afloat, the crew of the cargo ship lowered their lifeboats and rowed away from the ship. The second officer in one of the lifeboats watched the submarine gun crew wait until their boat got out of the way before pouring shells into their ship until it sank.

With their deadly job finished, the submarine approached one of the lifeboats and held a brief conversation with the second mate. The commander, talking through an interpreter among his men, asked if it was an American ship. The officer answered that it was. When asked what kind of a ship, he simply answered, "An American merchantman."

The U-boat commander did not appear to be in any hurry. He asked the Americans if there was anything he could do for them. There was. A wounded man was in the lifeboat, and the commander passed over some medical supplies. Then the second officer asked for the direction to the nearest land, and he was told to steer with the wind.

Looking at the submarine somewhat askance from their lifeboat, the American seamen noticed an insignia painted on the conning tower. It was a lioness standing on a hind foot. One of the front paws held a hammer and the tail carried a torch.

The lifeboat steered with the wind and reached Antigua a week later.

The Dutch island of Aruba with its vast oil tanks made an excellent target for the Caribbean gun crews. One day U-156, commanded by Korvettenkapitän Hartenstein, surfaced to fire on the huge tanks. The gunnery officer waited for some people to pass by, obviously on their way to church. In the meantime, he absentmindedly forgot to pull out the plug in the muzzle of the gun. When the gun went off, it exploded and injured the gunnery officer's leg. That particular operation ended in failure, but the gun was sawed off and later sank a ship. The wounded officer did not do so well. His leg grew worse and he was left on the island of Martinique for medical attention.

The gentlemanly ways of Hartenstein and his crew would prove disastrous. Later in the year, in the South Atlantic, Hartenstein torpedoed the *Laconia*, a British troopship. To his shock and consternation, he learned that many of the men foundering in the water were crying out in Italian. Plucking a large number of them out of the sea, he discovered the disturbing news that 1,700 Italian prisoners of war were on their way to North Africa. Also on board were eighty women and children, as well as hundreds of British troops and the crew, and some Polish ex-POWs of Russia. In dismay, Hartenstein offered aid to as many as possible. Hundreds were in the water, and his boat could take only a handful. He radioed headquarters for instructions.

Hartenstein was in a dangerous and delicate position. His overloaded boat could not dive, and he was an easy mark for an attack. Merely caring for so many survivors, among them many British, was an enormous, unwanted task. By the next morning he had about 400 charges scattered in surrounding lifeboats and on his boat. In desperation, he sent out a message in English on the international shipping distress band. It said, "If any ship will assist the shipwrecked *Laconia* crew I will not attack her, provided I am not attacked by ship or air force. I picked up 193 men 04.52S 11.26W German submarine."

Doenitz ordered the nearest U-boats to suspend their operations and go to the rescue. He worried about the safety of his boats, but he said to his staff who were not all in agreement with his actions, "I cannot put these people into the water."

For three days after the attack, Hartenstein made all kinds of makeshift arrangements. U-506 and U-507 arrived on the scene, and their crews pitched in, too. At night U-507 took as many women and children on board as could squeeze into the boat, and the crew gave them a warm meal, drinks, clothing, and medical attention.

During these tumultuous days, two French warships and an Italian ship arrived to help. No British ships made an appearance.

On the fourth day an American Liberator flew overhead, and the pilot looked down on the distress below. He saw a U-boat with fifty people on deck circled by four lifeboats. A large Red Cross flag waved from the U-156.

The perplexed pilot radioed the U. S. Naval Air Base on Ascension Island and in return received a command to attack the submarine.

The order from the base, seemingly inhumane, was more likely the result of suspicion about the situation. Limited communication caused lack of understanding, which in turn inadvertently caused cruel acts. At best, wars are inhumane affairs. The sole aim of destroying the enemy closed the mind to decency in unusual conditions. Undoubtedly the base commander feared a trap and envisioned the overriding opportunity to kill another deadly submarine.

Although the Liberator bombs did not hit U-156, they were close enough to force Hartenstein to evacuate the survivors from his boat so that he could dive.

Every aspect of the incident was tragic. The sad story convinced Doenitz once and for all that no more attempts could be made to save or extend aid to survivors. On September 17, 1942, he sternly ordered U-boat commanders to cease all such efforts unless there was an extenuating circumstance for gaining worthwhile intelligence. Their primary objective, he reminded them, was to destroy enemy ships and crews. He ended his message by saying, "Be severe. Remember that in his bombing attacks on German cities the enemy has no regard for women and children."

As the year wore on, U-boats found tougher opposition even in the Caribbean. Stiff training in antisubmarine tactics was beginning to show results. Air and sea attacks were better coordinated. Kapitänleutnant Otto Ites, in U-94, had a long record of success. Nevertheless, he was the victim of improved enemy operations between air and sea units. While patrolling in an area between Guantanamo Bay, Cuba, and Key West, Florida, he was sighted by a navy PBY seaplane. Depth charges from the aircraft brought the sub to the surface, and then two British corvettes working in harmony with the PBY added the final touches. One corvette arrived just as the U-boat came up, rammed it twice, and dropped more depth charges to finish U-94.

In another part of the world U-boats continued to produce effective results. This area was along the Allied convoy route to the embattled Soviet Union. During these hard days, the convoy assignment that men feared the most was the run to Murmansk or Archangel, far above the Arctic Circle. Danger threatened the merchant ships from every direction. U-boats were only one threat. There was always the possibility of an attack from heavy surface ships such as the battleship *Tirpitz* or from the Luftwaffe base in Norway. The desperate straits of the Russians made the risk necessary, but the Allies answered their pleas for help with the utmost reluctance.

In March 1942 the *Tirpitz* had actually sunk a straggling merchant ship. Convoy PQ 13 lost six ships from a combined air and destroyer action. Other convoys had heavy losses, and while defending themselves the British lost two cruisers, *Edinburgh* and *Trinidad*.

PQ 16 set out for Murmansk in May and fought off 108 waves of Luftwaffe attacks. Although the convoy delivered 250,000 tons of military supplies, eight merchant ships were sunk. The shipping rate on this route was estimated to be the highest for any route during the war.

In June PQ 17 departed from Iceland for Murmansk with twenty-two American and twelve other Allied ships. The heavily escorted convoy soon ran into the expected opposition. For three days planes bombed and strafed the ships unceasingly. Then the threat of the *Tirpitz* coming out to intercept the convoy prompted the first sea lord, Admiral Sir Dudley Pound, to order the group to scatter. In doing so, he made a bad mistake.

The *Tirpitz* did not come out to attack, but the unprotected ships that had scattered were now at the mercy of both U-boats and aircraft. Only eleven ships reached

Murmansk. Tens of thousands of tons of military supplies, thousands of vehicles, hundreds of tanks, and more than 200 planes being transported went to the bottom of the sea.

This setback halted convoys to northern Russia until September when PQ 18 made another attempt without much more success. The same story repeated itself. The U-boats and Luftwaffe took their toll. Thirteen ships in a convoy of forty were sunk. The Murmansk run had not become any easier.

Still another area of operation, the South Atlantic, produced substantial victories for Doenitz. In the fall of 1942 six boats made the long run to Cape Town, and it was a profitable voyage for the Germans. The results off the African coast sounded like another happy time. Lüth, Merton, Emmermann, and Ibekken were among the commanders who did themselves proud. Even the wounded Creamer, commander of U-333, reached home safely when his very young third officer took control in the emergency.

Despite occasional difficulties, 1942 was another good year for the U-boats. The construction program added a stream of new boats each month, and the number of sinkings continued to climb. By November the U-boats had set a new record. A total of 117 ships, amounting to more than 700,000 tons, were sunk in that month alone. Nonetheless, the "second happy time" was soon over. Doenitz must have noticed a danger signal as he studied his charts. The tonnage sunk by each U-boat started to go down even though the total amount was impressive.

In the winter of 1942–43 the U-boat operations would shift back to the mid-Atlantic, and the biggest battles were still to come. By now even Hitler knew that his first line of defense was in the Atlantic. There was certainly no cause for gloom yet. The successes heavily outweighed the losses, and in January 1943 Doenitz replaced Raeder as commander in chief of the Kriegsmarine. As Raeder's influence with Hitler faded with the failure of his surface ships, Doenitz's influence with the fuehrer increased. As head of the navy, however, Doenitz did not let go of his grasp of the U-boat arm.

7

SABOTEURS

Late in May 1942 two German boats, U-584 and U-202, left Lorient for the American coast. This time, however, their chief mission was not to sink ships, but to carry saboteurs across the Atlantic and land them safely in the United States.

War generates wild schemes and plots. One of the wilder Nazi schemes was to land saboteurs on the East Coast of the United States to create general confusion.

To the officers of the Abwehr, the German intelligence agency led by Admiral Wilhelm Canaris, the plan seemed perfectly sensible. They selected for this special mission men who had lived in the United States, spoke good English, and knew American ways. After intensive training in explosives and the secret tricks of sabotage, a few men, they thought, could cause considerable mischief, slow industrial production, and demoralize the people.

Special assignments for U-boats always annoyed Doenitz. They only distracted him from his primary objective, which was to sink merchant ships. Although he went along with the project, he had little use for Canaris who, he said, never supplied him with any worthwhile intelligence. The leaders of the U-boat arm developed their own information without waiting for Canaris.

At any rate, U-584 departed first, on May 26, for the Florida coast. Two days later U-202 left for Long Island. Each boat carried four saboteurs who were well financed to do their dirty work. The leader of each group had ninety thousand dollars to use as he saw fit.

After sixteen days at sea, U-202 arrived off Amagansett, a sparsely populated area at the eastern end of Long Island with miles of empty, lonely, unprotected beach.

The passengers on U-202 had not enjoyed their voyage. The close quarters, the dives to escape destroyers, and the frightening depth charges were not for them. As they reached their landing area, the tension was high, even though they must have felt a sense of relief to leave the miserable boat.

A crew member rowed the four men to shore in a rubber boat and then returned to the submarine. The four men were Georj Dasch, the leader; Ernest Burger; Richard Quirin; and Heinrich Heinck. The landing went well. The night was dark, fog hung low overhead, and the beach was deserted. The men quickly took off the German uniforms that they wore in case they were immediately caught. As military men they would have been taken as prisoners of war, not shot as spies. No one was in sight, so it seemed safe enough to make the change.

Dasch was already in his civilian clothes when out of the darkness a young man appeared. He was twenty-one-year-old Coast Guardsman John C. Cullen, walking his solitary patrol. Each night, without a gun, he covered a stretch of beach three miles each way, looking for signs of any strange activity. He had never seen anything amiss.

Both the Germans and the American were completely taken aback. Instinctively, Cullen sensed something odd as he turned his flashlight on the men and asked who they were.

Dasch, trying to be friendly, said, "We're fishermen from Southampton [a nearby town], and we ran aground here." Dasch claimed that his name was George Davis. The story was plausible until one of the men in the black background said something in what sounded to Cullen like German. Dasch told the man to shut up.

Cullen, using his head, said that the men ought to go with him to the Coast Guard station for the night and take care of their boat in the morning. Then the attitude of the stranger changed.

Dasch said, "I don't want to kill you." But the implication was the exact opposite. The threat was clear to Cullen. Next, Dasch offered Cullen $150 to forget the whole incident and in almost the same breath raised the amount to $300. The unarmed Cullen wisely took the money and rushed back to his station to report the incredible incident.

Dasch and his cohorts also hurried from the scene. Had their bribe worked? No one knew. It would probably have been better to kill the young man and dispose of the body.

Cullen excitedly told his story to Boatswain's Mate Carl Jenette and gave him the money, which amounted to $260, not $300. He had been shortchanged. Jenette phoned Warrant Officer Warren Barnes, the commander of the station, and then took off with Cullen and three other men to check the area. As they approached the spot, they smelled diesel oil, heard the sound of an engine, and then saw a submarine. The U-202 had grounded and was working itself off. Soon the boat vanished.

In the light of day there was no question that weird happenings had taken place the night before. The saboteurs may have graduated from an intensive training course, but they carelessly left plenty of evidence behind. Buried in the sand were four wooden boxes of explosives and a duffel bag with German uniforms. On the beach someone had also left a pack of German cigarettes. Cullen's imagination was certainly not working overtime.

By now, Naval Intelligence and the FBI had been notified, and agents swarmed all over eastern Long Island. Some worked in the vicinity as undercover men to no avail. There was no sign of the invaders.

The four Germans had taken the Long Island Railroad to New York City where they registered at two hotels and began to enjoy some of the best restaurants in the city. Meanwhile, U-548 landed its group of saboteurs at Ponte Vedra, Florida. No one saw them come ashore, and at daylight, wearing swimming trunks, they mingled with the other bathers without attracting any attention. Two of the men, Edward Kerling and Werner Thiel, left for New York. The other two, Herbert Haupt and Hermann Neubauer, went to Chicago.

The men were in no hurry to carry out their assignment. Dasch had already proven that he was not a killer, and now he thought about giving up the entire project. He was married to a native American and did not really want to go ahead with the plan. His next step was to sound out Burger who seemed receptive when he said he intended to call the FBI and reveal everything. Burger may have been amazed by Dasch, but he offered no objection and became his ally.

Burger had his own reasons for abandoning the mission. Although he had been a member of the German-American Bund, a Nazi-inspired organization, during his years in the United States, he had become a citizen and had actually served in the Michigan National Guard. That had not prevented him from becoming a disgruntled citizen, however, and he had returned to Germany to seek a better way of life under the Nazis. At first, he became a storm trooper and his brutal future as a bully boy for Hitler seemed ensured. He was even acquainted with the fuehrer. Nevertheless, he became trapped in the internal politics of the ruthless Nazis and, as a victim of the gestapo, spent seventeen months in prison. His faith in Hitler's regime faded even while he joined the hazardous intelligence group. To the Nazis, however, he appeared to be restoring himself in the eyes of the party.

The FBI agent on duty in the office on Federal Square in New York City was used to receiving crackpot calls and listening to weird, unfounded stories. The call from Dasch, from all indications, was another such call. Still, the agent dutifully reported the conversation. Dasch told him that he had arrived from Germany and that he intended to get in touch with the Washington office of the FBI within the next few days. He said that he had important information that he could reveal only to the director, J. Edgar Hoover. The FBI man asked about the nature of the information, but Dasch hung up.

True to his word, Dasch showed up in Washington, checked in at the luxurious Mayflower Hotel, and phoned the FBI. This time he admitted that he was one of the German saboteurs. The agent on the other end of the line was aware of the Amagansett affair. In a few brief minutes, agents descended on Dasch in his hotel room and took him to their office.

Dasch still wanted to see Hoover. Frustrated in that attempt, he divulged all details of the plot to the agents and surprised them with the news that a second landing had taken place in Florida.

By now, no one doubted Dasch's strange tale. The evidence found on the Long Island beach supported him. The explosives, as Dasch said, looked like pieces of coal. They were to be used in industrial furnaces. The main targets were to have been plants, especially those that produced aluminum. Of lesser importance were fire bombs for hotels, department stores, and other public places to stir panic among the people. In addition, Dasch gave the FBI a handkerchief with invisible writing. It contained the names of two contacts in America and the address of a

Lisbon mail drop for communicating with the German intelligence agency.

Although the intensive investigation of the past few days on Long Island had been fruitless, the FBI now had the whole story handed to them.

Dasch and his comrade Burger had expected to be received as heroes by the Americans. Now they saw their dreams of glory collapse. The warmth of the American people did not extend to these two Nazis. Instead, they ended up in prison. And before the end of the month all members of the two sabotage groups that they had betrayed were behind bars.

Once in custody, thirty-three-year-old Kerling, who once had been a chauffeur for rich Americans, showed agents where they had buried their cache under the Florida sands. Apparently they had done a better job of hiding their wares.

Kerling, Quirin, Heinck, and Thiel had been rounded up immediately. That left two men at large: Neubauer and Haupt. The FBI located Haupt in Chicago and gave him a loose rein for a few days. They wanted to get a line on his activities and let him lead them to Neubauer, who had once been a cook in Chicago.

Haupt, an American citizen who, like Burger, had been an ardent member of the German-American Bund, had been employed at one time as an optical worker in Chicago. As the FBI agents tailed him, they found that this dedicated Nazi, like his associates, was in no hurry to blow up America. Instead, he chased women, spent hours in the movies, and generally dawdled away his time. By June 27 both Haupt and Neubauer were under arrest.

Certainly the Abwehr had selected a sorry lot of men to carry out such a mission. Their behavior supported Doenitz's view that Canaris and his agency were incompetent.

The American people were unaware of this threat to their country until the news broke after the men had been captured, and even then they did not learn the full story.

Nothing was told about the voluntary admissions of Dasch. Instead, newspapers based their stories on press releases from the FBI and reported the activities in the most heroic and glamorous manner. Once again, the public was informed, agents had unraveled a great mystery.

The wartime mood of the President and attorney general, as well as the nation, left little room for mercy for these sinister intruders. There was no public trial. Under a veil of secrecy, the saboteurs were tried by court martial. The betrayers, Dasch and Burger, received life sentences and after the war were deported to Germany. The remaining six were electrocuted.

The daring, ill-conceived, and poorly executed plan ended in disaster for the Nazis and put an end to the Abwehr's sabotage efforts in America for a long time to come. Doenitz would not be distracted for some time by missions of this sort. The affair also served as a warning to America that such things could happen. A less inept, more determined group of desperadoes could have succeeded in doing real damage within the borders of the United States.

8

WOLF PACKS

The wolf packs grew in strength, their coordination improved with experience, and they were having a heyday by late 1942. Doenitz, still the mastermind, skillfully maneuvered his boats into the most favorable position to strike. As the Allies shifted convoy routes and added escorts, Doenitz analyzed their moves and anticipated their methods. He was firmly convinced that he had to orchestrate the wolf packs from his central location. It saved time, fuel, and effort. No one could argue that he had not achieved impressive results.

Doenitz had a source of information not available to his boat commanders that sometimes made him look like a mind reader. The highly secret work of radio interceptors and cryptographers on the staff of the naval high command was passed along to him. Few people knew of the painstaking work of this small group of technicians who frequently broke British radio codes. Their success was astounding, but early in the war their information did not always reach Doenitz in time to be useful. By mid-1942, however, they had improved their speed in breaking codes and forwarding to the U-boat arm invaluable information about convoy routes.

The number of U-boats at sea also increased dramatically. The construction program that had been slow at the start now produced twenty to thirty new boats a month. U-boat losses continued, but the mortality rates were taken for granted. The important thing was to keep the exchange rate favorable, and there were now a hundred or more boats at sea.

Still, there were dangers in Doenitz's central direction. All major decisions were in his hands. To make those decisions he needed information from his commanders. He had to receive word of their sightings and relay messages to other boats in the area. Radio was the only means of communication, and every time a commander used his radio he faced the danger of detection. Nonetheless, that was the system, it worked well, and Doenitz was gaining in Hitler's favor.

By late fall two groups of U-boats were available at all times in the North Atlantic to engage the convoys. One patrolled the eastern Atlantic and the other the western Atlantic off the Grand Banks of Newfoundland. With additional boats, the distance between each boat on patrol was cut down to only fifteen or twenty miles. For a convoy to escape the U-boat network required luck, magic, or plenty of skill. Sometimes twenty boats attacked a convoy at the same time, and the engagements often dragged on for a week or more and covered a thousand miles. When the wolves had the scent, they did not let go.

Doenitz was so insistent on sinking enemy ships in the North Atlantic that he missed one of the great opportunities of the war. He was no superman, and he made his share of costly mistakes. Perhaps one of the worst was to be caught off guard when 350 Allied cargo vessels and troopships and 200 warships crossed the mid-Atlantic at the end of October without the U-boats touching them. Operation Torch, the American invasion of North Africa, was under way. No wonder Doenitz despised the intelligence chief, Admiral Canaris. But it was his fault, too. He was caught napping.

In a last minute effort, Doenitz sent fifteen submarines to attack the Allied amphibious force. He accomplished little. The Americans had set up a strong antisubmarine defense in the landing area, and the water was too shallow for effective U-boat operations. The U-boats were badly battered. Two were lost and six seriously damaged.

The U-boat losses off North Africa gave Doenitz an opportunity to defend himself. He insisted, as he had before, that his mission was to sink merchant shipping and destroy the lifelines of trade. His successes spoke for themselves, and he was now sufficiently entrenched with Hitler to protect his position. No one would shake him from his determination to concentrate on the North Atlantic.

Gales swept across the North Atlantic during the winter of 1942–43. The previous winter had been bad, but this was the worst in fifty years. Once more the elements were as troublesome as the enemy. Both sides suffered from the raging seas, but for all the discomfort and danger, the U-boats continued to harass the convoys. Some Allies who endured the ordeal called it the "bloody winter."

The foul weather seemed everlasting. On the surface, a boat had to keep its hatch open for fast dives, and water rushed into it as the vessel rocked from side to side. Below, the normally putrid smells became worse as humidity rotted the food. The unclean crewmen became more obnoxious as their bodies and clothes increased their rank odors.

Even the best sailors sickened with the endless swaying of the boats, and on deck they were pelted with snow, sleet, and ocean spray. The boats pitched and rolled, pitched and rolled. The unrelenting wind cut into the men's faces despite

The commander of U-86 in May or June 1942. (PHOTO: BUNDESARCHIV)

the masks they wore to protect their skin. Even when lashed to stanchions with steel belts, some men were torn from the boats and thrown into the sea.

Captains and crews in the convoys fared little better. Some escort ships rolled fifty degrees on each side, and men wondered if their ship would ever right itself again. Radar was a helpless blur in the extreme storms, and captains continually had to worry about collisions. Some merchant ships broke in half from the steady pounding of the sea. The crews suffered from the wintry blasts, but there was always the hope that the nasty weather might hide them from the U-boats.

Convoy commodores and escort commanders had good reason to hope that they might evade the enemy. Usually it was a matter of hope against hope, yet once in a while they were lucky. In January Doenitz received solid intelligence reports about eastbound convoy HX 223. He sent fifteen U-boats to intercept and destroy it southeast of Greenland. Near the point of juncture, hurricane-strength winds with mountainous 60-foot waves and poor visibility broke up the attack. The convoy sailed through the patrol unseen and unharmed. It was truly an ill wind that blew some good.

Allied air patrols were grounded during this miserable weather, and even in good weather their range was limited. No plane could cover the entire Atlantic, and this left a big gap in the middle where merchantmen and escort seaman held their breath and prayed for the best. They called the unprotected area "the black pit."

A few days after the good fortune of HX 223, another convoy, HX 224, also escaped considerable damage. Nevertheless, the U-boats sank three ships, and the U-632 picked up a survivor from a tanker. Through stupidity, weakness, or treachery, the unheroic seaman told the U-boat commander that a slow convoy, SC 118, was two days behind them sailing the same route. This information substantiated reports that Doenitz had received from cryptographers, and he moved his boats into position for another attack.

Leaving Halifax, SC 118 consisted of sixty-three ships. In the escort were three British destroyers, three British corvettes, a Free French corvette, and the U.S. Coast Guard cutter *Bibb*.

Convoy SC 118 should have been a sitting duck for the U-boats. Aside from the radio interception and the survivor's treacherous revelation, a merchantman had accidentally fired a flare that gave their position away.

By a fluke, the convoy slipped by sixteen U-boats lying in wait during the night. U-187 spotted the flare from the merchant ship, but an alert destroyer sank the submarine. For three days the escorts held the wolves at bay and badly damaged some of them. It was a remarkable combination of luck, skill, toughness, and determination. This was a running battle, however, and such favorable circumstances could not be counted on to last indefinitely.

Prowling the North Atlantic at the moment was the bright and daring Baron von Forstner. He had learned a lot since his disappointing days in the South Atlantic. Recently he had chalked up a number of successes, and he was no longer a novice skipper. In five patrols he had built up an enviable record. The aristocrat had proven his mettle. Now, the appearance of a large convoy gave him a chance to climb into the realm of the top aces. Much of the time the boats were operating in the black pit, and he was confident that he and his fellow wolves could run up a sizable score.

Von Forstner, in U-402, rushed at top speed toward the columns of ships in SC 118, and so did nineteen other U-boats. When the baron approached the convoy, its escorts had left the starboard side to track down the enemy. The gap they left was wide enough to open a hole for U-402 to enter. Without any trouble, von Forstner sank a small ship that turned out to be the convoy's rescue vessel, *Toward*, a vital unit. He missed his second target on the first try and then made up for it on the second effort. A tanker was hit and burning. The baron, however, wanted nothing left undone. There was a question in his mind as to whether or not the tanker was mortally wounded, so he crept closer and inflicted a fatal blow.

The U-614 added further confusion in the midst of SC 118. Attacking from the port side, the submarine sank a straggling cargo ship that was vainly trying to escape the action.

The attacks had taken only twenty minutes, and the loss of the rescue ship added to the consternation. Some escorts had to take time out from hunting submarines to search for survivors. Only two escorts remained to protect the convoy from further sinkings. Then, because of a mix-up in signals, the escort commander received a false notion of the position of his ships. Star shells and searchlights swept over the sea in search of submarines and survivors. Desperate efforts caused near-collisions that increased the nerve-wracking tension.

Von Forstner thrived on the confusion. He sank another tanker. Some of his fellow commanders were not so fortunate. Escorts hounded U-262, for one, and succeeded in damaging it.

The U-609, under the command of Kapitänleutnant Rudloff, had the misfortune of moving into the vicinity of the Free French corvette *Lobelia* at the wrong moment. The little ship picked up the submarine on radar and hurried to close the range. Within 3,500 yards the *Lobelia* fired star shells, and the captain, Lieutenant Pierre Morsier, got a good look at his adversary. Still closer, he started firing his machine guns, and the U-boat dived. The *Lobelia* followed the sub with a sound contact. Rudloff's maneuvering under the sea did not throw off the persistent escort. Morsier made a depth charge run, and then another. It was the end for Rudloff and his crew. The undersea explosions left no room for doubt that U-609 was gone.

No sooner had the U-609 exploded than the escort *Abelia* received a submarine contact. The wolves were everywhere. *Abelia* attacked, and another U-boat was out of the fight.

The wolf pack faced a determined foe, and the battle proved costly to them. They could no longer shrug off the escorts as inept and ineffective. Still, the more daring U-boat commanders penetrated the screen and hour after hour ran up and down the convoy columns creating havoc. Torpedoes found their mark, shells crashed into ships. Men on both sides, near exhaustion, refused to give up.

Von Forstner knew from the underwater sounds that Rudloff was lost. He knew that he could be next, and yet nothing stopped him. He found another gap in the screen and inside the convoy sank two more ships in the early morning hours.

At about 0600 von Forstner, still on the bridge, sighted a ship in the distance. He called out to his crew that it was a freighter of about 9,000 tons. Actually, it was the 6,000-ton *Henry Mallory*, which carried a valuable cargo of almost four hundred army, navy, and marine corps personnel to Iceland.

The fairly fast 14-knot *Mallory*, for some unknown reason, had been assigned to the slow 7-knot convoy. Now, the *Mallory* was straggling astern of the convoy. The strange behavior of the ship, sailing on a straight course without zigzagging, almost invited attack.

Von Forstner quickly sized up the situation. His men made calculations, and then he gave the order to fire a torpedo. One torpedo was all that was needed.

Nothing seemed to go right on the *Mallory*. Most of the passengers and crew might have survived. There was sufficient time to lower the boats in an orderly way, but panic spread and increased the death toll. No directions came from the bridge. No SOS went out on the radio, no signal went up, and the order to abandon ship was never given. It was every man for himself, a situation that hurt everyone. Working together, the crew should have been able to launch the lifeboats in the rough sea. Instead, almost half of the lifeboats failed to get away safely. Lowering boats always required care. That night three boats turned over on the way down; one of them was filled with wounded men.

Heads bobbed everywhere in the water, but their pain and anguish would soon be over. No one could last long in the near-freezing temperatures. Men froze on the rafts, and only those in the lifeboats had a relatively safe haven.

As frequently happened, there were unusual stories of escape. One army officer jumped into the sea at the last minute as the ship was going down. He later admitted that he had felt sheer panic during his jump, but when he came to the surface he threw up and then felt better. He saw some wreckage floating by, climbed onto it, and was eventually picked up.

No one in the convoy knew that the *Mallory* had gone down, so no ships rushed to help. About four hours after von Forstner's sighting, the Coast Guard cutter *Bibb*, chasing contacts, ran across a boatload of survivors. The captain, Commander Ray Raney, started rescue operations and notified other ships. Sadly they found many lifeless bodies in the water.

The cutter *Ingham* joined the search. Again, the heroism of men, not recognized then or later, was amazing that morning. Volunteers jumped into the *Ingham* lifeboat led by Lieutenant John Waters. Once clear of the ship, Waters directed the boat toward the heads in the water. One body after another was lifeless. It was a gruesome job, and there was also a good possibility that they would lose sight of their ship and be no better off than the men they hoped to save. Nevertheless, they rowed onward and pulled three soldiers out of a swamped boat. Each of the three men had undergone exactly the same experience, yet one man was in far better condition than the other two. What had made the difference? Was it a matter of physical stamina or mental attitude? Some men apparently had a greater will to live.

After hours of hard work, the men realized that darkness was setting in. Waters's boat was filled with dead men, and some others who were more dead than alive, as he steered into the unknown. In the sea of bodies, Waters realized that he had no more room in his boat. He looked carefully at each man's eyes and decided whether or not they were alive. His hands were too frozen to feel a pulse. Sailors took off the ID tags of those who were declared dead and dropped them into the sea. Soon there was room in the boat for more survivors.

Finally, the *Ingham* showed up again and took the men on board. Despite the best efforts of all the late-arriving rescue teams, almost two-thirds of the men on the *Mallory* were lost.

The battle between the subs and the convoy had gone on for days. Still, von Forstner pursued the merchant ships.

In all he sank seven ships. Doenitz, following the struggle at headquarters, was well pleased with the young Prussian's results. He sent him an encouraging message:

> Forstner well done. Stay there and maintain contact. More boats are on the way. The depth charges also run out. Stay tough. This convoy is extremely important.

Von Forstner stayed tough, but the Coastal Command was now within range, and its aircraft forced the U-boats to submerge. One Liberator jumped the U-624, let go with three depth charges, and sank or severely damaged it. Yet, Doenitz was now almost rich with U-boats. When one was lost, it could be easily replaced.

The wolf packs were paying off. Doenitz thought that the battle against SC 118 was "perhaps the hardest fought battle of the whole war." It was also one of the most successful for the Germans. They had sunk thirteen ships in the convoy.

Von Forstner had been a standout. His days of frustration were over. Now he had sunk a total of more than 100,000 tons and received the Knight's Cross. The baron, never easy on his crew, remained quiet about his own triumphs and gave the credit to his men. Their morale reached a new high pitch, and the crew of U-402 became well known in the nightclubs near the sub bases. Their distinctiveness and camaraderie received a boost from the baroness. She made red pom-poms that they proudly wore on their hats.

The dark side of the battle against SC 118 for the Germans was that they had lost three boats and two others were damaged. It was true that they could be replaced, but inherent in the loss was the warning that Allied resistance was stiffening.

For the present the wolf packs caused the convoys giant-sized headaches. SC 118 was not the only convoy with high losses during that severe winter. Convoy after convoy arrived in Europe battered and bruised with big gaps in its columns.

In the first twenty days before the advent of spring, ninety-seven Allied ships were sent to the bottom. British maritime supremacy tottered under these heavy blows. When every minute carried a threat to life, time passed very slowly. It seemed as though these murderous sinkings would never stop.

In January 1943 President Roosevelt and Prime Minister Churchill met at Casablanca in North Africa with their military chiefs to discuss future strategy. They clearly recognized the U-boat destruction and decided to take steps to obliterate the menace of German submarines. The best way, they thought, was to attack the source of the problem. This meant bombing the sub bases on the French coast until there was nothing left of them. They were sure that would get at the root of the matter.

The Allied air strikes against the sub bases began in January and continued until May. Wave after wave of bombers dropped 19,000 tons of explosives on the German bases and supporting yards. It was a gigantic, determined effort aimed at the annihilation of the U-boat. Certainly this would settle the problem once and for all. But it did not.

The air strikes boomeranged on the Allies. In this energetic campaign, 262 Allied aircraft were lost, and not a single U-boat was destroyed. The engineers who had built the sub bases had done their work well. Bombs bounced off the concrete shelters and failed to pierce them. The heavily constructed pens proved impenetrable. When the raiders approached, the men sealed the submarine bunkers by lowering enormous steel doors. The docks and repair shops, with roofs 20 feet thick, were left undamaged. The bombings did not hurt the U-boat crews because they were housed in the country away from the bases.

Once more, a solution that seemed simple in theory had failed in practice. This air power, properly used to support the convoys, would undoubtedly have been more effective.

One analyst estimated that the planes might have made as many as seven hundred submarine sightings. Speculation was useless, however, because that just did not happen. During the worst days of the winter of 1942–43, only one squadron of Liberators, based in Iceland, covered the black pit in the mid-Atlantic.

9

COUNTERATTACK

The seemingly endless winter, like all winters, came to an end. The months of death and torment gave way to better weather. Once again, men hoped that they would be able to cope with the enemy without interference from gales and freezing temperatures.

The U-boat men had every expectation of success for the new year. In the last six months of 1942, mainly in well-coordinated wolf pack attacks, they had sunk more than two million tons of shipping. There was no reason to believe that the next months would not be just as successful.

Yet the war at sea had become more than a battle of skill among sailors. Allied and German scientists, working in their laboratories at home, also pitted their skills against one another. They, too, were playing a game of move and countermove. Both sides had encountered technical difficulties and disappointments in the early stages of the war. Scientists as well as seamen had to learn from their failures. None of them were ready to give up.

On the Allied side, the great achievement in antisubmarine warfare was radar. The first radar was crude and bulky and operated by men who needed more training and experience to utilize fully its vast potential. Time helped out. As the months rolled by, both the scientists and the seamen gained a better understanding of their new instrument. Research and development created new, improved models. Experience in battle taught dexterity in operation.

Radar was based on the reflection of radio waves from a solid surface back to a sending set. It projected on a screen the range and bearing of the object that it struck, and it worked just as well at night as in daytime. It was like a cat in the dark. Land-based radar stations had been a godsend in the Battle of Britain. But the early, massive, heavy, and complex units were difficult to install on ships. They took up so much space that they squeezed out other necessary equipment. Nevertheless, by the end of 1941 a few radar sets had been placed on Allied ships and had received limited use. They were little help against submarines because they could not usually pick up such a small target in the ocean. By the end of the next year, a new SG model appeared that was more accurate and had an increased range. As rapidly as possible, it was installed on all Allied naval ships, and eventually it turned the tide in submarine warfare.

At first, the use of radar on aircraft appeared to be impossible because of the weight and space requirements. Here too, scientists made refinements, and achieved what was once considered impossible. The first meter-wave radar on aircraft could sight a submarine far beyond anything that the pilot or the crew could see.

German scientists, renowned for their great ability, were caught off guard by radar, but they were not completely asleep. They counterattacked at the end of 1942 with a search receiver for U-boats. It cut down the effectiveness of meter-wave radar on aircraft.

The Allies realized that they could not rest on their scientific laurels. Nothing remained the same, and they knew that they must develop a microwave radar for aircraft.

A 10-centimeter set, developed by the Massachusetts Institute of Technology radiation laboratory, could not be detected by the U-boats' search receivers. With the arrival of the spring and summer of 1943, microwave radar in aircraft performed wonders in tracking down submarines and became the wolf packs' worst enemy. In another year, Hitler admitted that the invention blocked the success of his U-boats. German scientists, despite their worldwide reputation for excellence, never discovered a way to stop the 10-centimeter radar waves.

The Germans had no radar on their U-boats until the end of the war, and their countermeasures in 1943 were crude. Their first radar-warning equipment, installed in the fall of 1942, was called METOX. It was a bulky arrangement that was set on the conning tower after surfacing. A seaman rotated the antenna by hand, and rough bearings on radar signals were fixed. It was useful only on a long wavelength band and was worthless against shortwave radar. An improved system called NAXOS appeared at the end of 1943, but it, too, had limitations. In desperation, the Nazis tried cure-alls like special paint on the hull and nonreflecting material. None of them worked.

Radar was the most effective aid in the battle against U-boats, but it was not the only one. Although asdic—or sonar, as the Americans called it—had not worked miracles as the British had expected before the war, it was useful and was later improved. For a short time, it appeared that the Germans had the answer to sound search. They developed *Pillenwerfer*. The U-boats fooled Allied sound gear operators by shooting out innumerable small, stationary gas bubbles that tossed back an echo that sounded like a submarine. More than one sound man was tricked by the clever device, but improved training and improved sonar gear soon did much to undermine the effectiveness of *Pillenwerfer*.

A high-frequency direction finder, HF/DF, called "Huff-Duff," was another scientific aid of tremendous value to the Allies. Huff-Duff picked up radio transmissions from U-boats. The direction finders received cross-bearings when a submarine radioed back to base or to another submarine. The bearings were plotted, and the course of the submarine could be established. At first HF/DF systems were used only at shore stations. As early as the summer of 1942, the Naval Operating Base at Bermuda fixed the position of a submarine that led Lieutenant Richard Schreder, pilot of a navy patrol plane, to the U-158. The submarine was sunk without any survivors.

Doenitz, for all of his astuteness, made a basic mistake that cost the lives of many of his men. He used the radio too much. Under his system of operation he had placed himself at the center of affairs. It was necessary for the coordination of the wolf packs, but HF/DF was listening. Yet, he continued his use of radio until the end of the war. If he had been wiser, he would have insisted on radio silence or at least reduced radio messages before it was too late.

The increased number of antisubmarine ships carrying these improved weapons also made a difference. Dozens of new sub chasers that ranged in size from 110 to 180 feet were used with coastal convoys. More Coast Guard cutters and navy destroyers also appeared. The destroyers were the most powerful and effective antisubmarine ships. The *Fletcher*, a class destroyer, was 376 feet long and slashed through the water at speeds up to 35 knots.

The depth charge, the weapon most frequently used against U-boats, also packed a bigger wallop as time passed. By the summer of 1943 a new depth charge sank faster to reach the target and carried Torpex, a more powerful explosive than the TNT previously used.

Since the sound contact always broke within 100 to 150

Sighting equipment on board U-86. (PHOTO: BUNDESARCHIV)

yards of the U-boat, there was a certain amount of guess-work in laying down an attack pattern. To minimize the uncertainty, the "hedgehog" fired twenty-four projectiles that were thrown up into the air and crashed into the sea before the sound contact was broken. They were often used with depth charges.

With many of these scientific advances coming into actual use, new hope arrived for the Allies in the spring of 1943.

Von Forstner learned about the tougher tactics of the Allies the hard way. That same spring he attacked convoy SC 129 in his usual efficient manner. Then, the tables turned, and he took a terrible beating in a depth charge attack. His boat went out of control and plummeted beneath the test depth. Was this the end for one of the few remaining aces? The skillful von Forstner checked the dive, but the hammering of depth charges went on and on. Even the cool commander's confidence was shaken. He called his men together in the control room and led them in prayer.

There was nothing else to do except prepare for the end. Then, after what seemed an eternity, the depth charges stopped. The escort ships had lost contact with their prey. The end had not yet come, and von Forstner slowly limped back to the base at La Pallice. He had completed his seventh patrol.

In April, Commander Sloop Berdine, commanding officer of the U.S. Coast Guard cutter *Spencer,* received an asdic contact while escorting a convoy. He dropped depth charges, and the U-boat dived under the convoy. The *Spencer* chased the submarine and fired a hedgehog pattern that caused the boat to come to the surface. Heavy gunfire opened up on both sides, and a navy armed guard crew on one of the merchant ships got a rare hit on a sub. The U-boat's situation became hopeless, and the men dived into the sea.

The *Spencer* had lost one man in the exchange of gunfire, and seven others were wounded. Now the cutter started on a course to ram the submarine. As the ship closed in, the captain realized that no one was on the submarine. Instead of sinking the boat, he thought, perhaps he could capture it.

Berdine ordered Lieutenant Ross Bullard to take a party of men and board the boat, not exactly an easy assignment. Bullard took a .45 automatic pistol and a bag of hand grenades and was the first man to reach the conning tower. Not knowing what he would find below, he threw a grenade down the hatch. When the smoke cleared, he climbed down the ladder and found three dead men who were probably killed in the earlier battle. No one else was on board.

Bullard had plenty of guts. Descending the ladder he could easily have been shot by remaining members of the crew. Perhaps the greater danger was the real possibility that he might go down with the boat. There was no question that it was sinking. A quick look around told him that the boat was too far gone to become a prize of war.

The courageous lieutenant came up on deck without a moment to spare and jumped into the water as the U-boat went down. He may not have captured the boat, but he was the first American to board an operating enemy ship at sea in more than a hundred years.

With the hope of capturing the U-boat dashed, Berdine turned to picking up survivors. The Germans had little to say to their rescuers, and the German officers went to the extreme of not giving even their rank and serial number. The highest-ranking surviving officer was Lieutenant zur See Peter Paul Moeller. There was little communication between the Germans and the Americans, partly because of the Germans' sullenness and partly because of the language problem. Yet when he got off the *Spencer* in Ireland, Moeller, who had given the impression of not knowing any English, thanked Berdine in perfect English for the care that he and his crew had received.

By the end of the next month, Doenitz faced graver problems. The U-boat war that had been going so well took a sudden disastrous turn. During May, escort ships sank one submarine after another. Their success was the result of hard work and dedication plus the accumulated effect of all the scientific advances. Radar, Huff-Duff, and improved asdic helped. The Allies also reaped the benefits of more escorts and increased air power.

As Doenitz studied his wall maps and charts, he noticed each day that the little pins with flags indicating submarines became fewer and fewer. Each day boats failed to respond to radio messages, and after a lapse of time they were presumed lost. How could this be? How could the situation reverse itself from good to bad in such a short time?

By May 1943 forty-one U-boats, one-third of the German submarines at sea, had been sunk. The tide of war in the

Atlantic had turned. One of the most successful aspects of a war to impose a totalitarian regime on the Western world was over. Although the collapse of the U-boats appeared to come quickly, it was the culmination of frantic effort by the Allies in the previous discouraging years. The courage, perserverance, and scientific ability of the Allies had enabled them to overcome staggering obstacles and prove that they were more than a match for the Third Reich.

At the time, this was beyond Doenitz's comprehension. He could not fully understand the drastic reversal. Was this another temporary setback? How could the Allies close in on his U-boats with such accuracy? It must be treason or espionage. In the Third Reich no one ever trusted anyone else anyway. Doenitz set in motion an intensive security check to find out who had betrayed the U-boat arm. Agents checked everywhere. They trailed the comings and goings of the U-boat staff, dug into their backgrounds, and failed to find the slightest evidence of betrayal. Finally, Doenitz said to his chief of staff after the series of investigations that they were the only two left who were not above suspicion.

One of more U-boats may have gone down as the result of intentionally careless work by French shipyard workers. That, however, was never the cause for the wholesale loss.

Doenitz may have underestimated the importance of radar for a while, and he failed to understand that his methods, once successful, were now proving fatal. His use of the radio, of course, played a big part in his undoing.

Controlling the North Atlantic was the key to cutting the Allied lifeline. That was fundamental. It was the principle that Doenitz had followed since the start of the war. Now, he had to retreat from his favorite battleground for a time. He had to regroup and reconsider his strategy. With a heavy heart he shifted his boats to the Central and South Atlantic. The war was not over. The U-boats continued to seek and destroy, but it was not the same war. The U-boats were no longer on the offensive.

A U-boat on patrol. (PHOTO: U.S. NAVY)

The increased air power continually forced the U-boats to submerge. Airplanes were now more than an irritation. They forced the boats to submerge for long periods, whereas they had once operated on the surface most of the time. Worse still, aircraft were actually sinking boats.

Springtime had brought better flying weather. More long-range planes could take off from Iceland to cover the mid-Atlantic black pit. More important, CVEs, the baby aircraft carriers, were now introduced as protectors of convoys. They were small ships, sometimes called jeep carriers that usually carried about twenty-four Wildcats and Avengers. The Wildcats, F4Fs, were fighter planes that could drop 500-pound bombs. The heavier Avengers, called TBFs, carried torpedoes, bombs, or depth charges.

The CVEs went a long way toward solving the problem of the black pit. Although weather sometimes kept the planes down, they usually gave convoys continuous air support. This new escort often produced phenomenal results. On May 19 Doenitz ordered two groups to form a patrol line of forty-two boats in an area between the Grand Banks and Greenland. Convoy ON 184, bound west, with the help of CVE *Bogue*, passed through this supposedly fool-proof U-boat line with surprising ease. As Avengers flew overhead, not a single ship in the convoy was lost.

The pilots on the little carriers deserved the highest praise for their courage. They faced two dangers each day they took off. One was the enemy; the other was the operational hazard. The risks of landing and taking off on the small flight deck caused the pilots much more concern than the Germans did. They were aware that operational casualties were high. Yet day in and day out they went about their job in the most businesslike way.

As the deadly month of May came to a close, Doenitz did his best to rally his men. He broadcast a message to the submarine officers to fight back. He said:

You alone can, at the moment, make an offensive attack against the enemy and beat him. The U-boat must, by continuous sinking of ships with war materiel and the necessary supplies for the British Isles, force the enemy to continual losses which must slowly but steadily sap the strength of the strongest force. The German people have long felt that our boats constitute the keenest and most decisive weapon and that the outcome of the war depends on the success or failure of the Battle of the Atlantic.

Doenitz was whistling in the dark. His only hope was that new scientific equipment would arrive in time to match the great strides made by the Allies. He extended that hope to his men when he went on to say:

The time will soon come in which you will be superior to the enemy with new and stronger weapons and will be able to triumph over your worst enemy—the aircraft and the destroyer.

His brave-sounding words had a hollow ring. The U-boat men realized that his message was actually an admission that they had lost supremacy in the Atlantic. They needed more than promises to beat the enemy. But they did not lose faith in Doenitz and continued to battle and hope that a better day would come.

During the summer of 1943 Doenitz decided to meet the problem of air power head on. His subs would no longer run away when aircraft appeared on the horizon. They would remain on the surface and fight back. To do this, he installed more antiaircraft guns on the boats and in the late fall many of them returned to the North Atlantic.

Doenitz's aggressiveness against air power proved to be one more bad mistake. His orders to shoot back were conscientiously carried out for about three months. During that time the situation only deteriorated. His gun crews shot down fifty-seven planes, which was no compensation for the twenty-eight submarines lost and twenty-two badly damaged from the air. With fifty boats out of commission, the order was rescinded.

The U-boat crews were not fully informed about these discouraging events. Those who were fortunate enough to return to base, however, could not help noticing the absence of comrades from other boats. Their morale was still high, but their sense of fatalism increased. Would their number be up next?

As the war went on, the life expectancy of the U-boat men grew shorter. Many did not return from their first patrol, and for a U-boat crew to survive more than three patrols was to beat the average. As the empty spaces were filled with new recruits, the young crews became even younger. Most of the enlisted men were now eighteen or nineteen, and the officers were in their early twenties. The average crew was a victim of its own inexperience, and the young commanders suffered in the knowledge that their background was insufficient.

The nature of the crews changed, too. During the early years of the war the U-boat men had prided themselves on their professionalism. They were not members of the Nazi party, and they considered themselves above politics. Now, many of the new recruits were ardent Nazis. Von Forstner noticed the difference. The young Nazis were quick to throw their weight around and assume authority, but he did not believe that they had an "accompanying sense of responsibility and self-control."

The shrill Nazi propaganda that increased as German military successes decreased also irritated von Forstner. When he was subjected to government lecturers who told him to hate the enemy, he felt that he had been insulted.

To regain the initiative, Doenitz needed more than propaganda. He needed air support. When his boats sailed from their bases on the French coast into the Bay of Biscay, they were immediately hounded by Allied aircraft. The bay itself was becoming a graveyard for U-boats. Goering gave Doenitz no comfort. The little air support that he received following his urgent requests was just not enough. This neglect by the Luftwaffe was inconceivable to Doenitz.

If the U-boats could not count on air protection, they would have to submerge for longer periods. The age-old problem haunted them. How could they recharge their batteries without coming up for air? Doenitz handed the problem to the scientists and expected an answer.

Doenitz also needed boats that could move faster undersea. The Type VII was an invaluable workhorse, but it became outmoded as modern warfare progressed in huge strides. A larger Type IX boat had been in operation for some time, but that, too, was slow.

Designers went to work at their drawing boards and came up with a new boat that could give them everything they needed. The plans were impressive. It would carry new radar plus antiradar devices. The sound gear would have a 50-mile range, and a supersonic-echo contrivance could determine the number of targets and their course, speed, and range. There would also be improved acoustic torpedoes. Perhaps most important, the boat could operate underwater at a speed of 19 knots and dive to 1,000 feet, below the range of depth charges.

All the scientific advances of the Allies could be overcome by this new boat, designated Type XXI. Once the plans were drawn, construction began without delay. This answer to the German problems could change defeat into victory at sea. Certainly these revolutionary boats could reestablish the supremacy of the U-boat in the Atlantic. Construction, however, took time. For now, U-boat crews would have to struggle with the Type VII and Type IX boats with a few new adaptations added.

The recent effectiveness of Allied air power was clearly shown in the fall of 1943. U-boats on the surface were pounced on at any time of day or night. They were particularly susceptible to attack when they rendezvoused with supply boats. The carrier pilots became adept at finding these supply points and sinking the boats while they were in the process of refueling.

At the end of July, Kapitänleutnant Horst Holtring, commander of U-604, was on patrol off Brazil when his boat was sighted by a shore-based Ventura aircraft. The pilot, Lieutenant Commander Thomas Davies, swooped down and straddled the boat with four bombs. Holtring crash-dived, and Davies was sure that he had sunk the boat. He was wrong. Somehow Holtring brought the badly damaged boat to the surface and radioed for help.

Arrangements were made for U-172 and U-185 to meet U-604 in a few days. Again, the use of radio gave the boats away, and Liberators attacked the three boats on the morning of August 3. Then the destroyer *Moffett* found the damaged U-604 in the evening, fired at it, and dropped two depth charges. Still, U-604 survived.

At 0426 the next day, U-604 surfaced only to be hounded by the *Moffett* again. Holtring used a new trick. He had a radar decoy on board called an "Aphrodite." It was a balloon that trailed plates covered with tinfoil that deceived radar operators. Holtring launched the gadget, and it worked. He had outwitted everyone once again.

Nevertheless, Holtring was still in trouble. He set a new rendezvous with U-185 and U-172 for the next week. In the meantime, U-185 was attacked and barely escaped.

On August 11 Lieutenant Commander B. J. Prueher, commander of a Liberator squadron, flew right into a hornet's nest. He had discovered the meeting place for the three boats that were busy making transfers. The commanders had decided to scuttle U-604, and the other boats were to split up the crew between them.

When Prueher attacked, the U-172 submerged while U-185 and U-604 fired on the plane. Unfortunately, Prueher's bombs missed, and the antiaircraft fire destroyed his plane. With the Liberator out of the way, the boats carried out their transfers and sank U-604. When completed, the two boats set out for their home base.

Holtring boarded U-185. On the way home, Lieutenant (j.g.) M. G. O'Neill, a carrier pilot, sighted the submarine and made a coordinated attack with the help of other aircraft. The combined effort succeeded, and the boat started to go down.

Holtring had been lying in a bunk when the shooting started. He got up, took his pistol, and went into the forward torpedo room where two men from his own boat were crying out in pain. Water had already flooded the battery compartment, and chlorine gas filled the air. The severely injured men begged Holtring to shoot them. He did, and then he shot himself. He could take no more.

The luckier U-172 arrived home with twenty-three of Holtring's men. But by the end of the year, U-172 would be gone, the victim of an air and sea attack.

Von Forstner, operating north of the Azores, had been at sea for weeks and was on his way to meet a supply boat. At about noon on October 13, Lieutenant Commander Howard Avery, pilot of a TBF from the U.S.S. *Card*, a CVE, sighted the submarine. He did not have any bombs, so he radioed for help. Another TBF, piloted by Ensign B. C. Sheela, appeared and took the U-402 by surprise. Sheela dropped a bomb that may have missed, but the boat dived. This gave Avery a chance to use a new MK homing torpedo that was not any use for a surface attack. The torpedo found its target. The U-402, the commander, and the crew, veterans of too many encounters, were gone.

The *milch cows* had been one of the important components of the U-boat arm. They had operated efficiently. Now, by the end of the summer, only three of the twelve *milch cows* survived. Doenitz wrote that no more supply boats were available. It was a significant loss that cut short his entire operation in the Central Atlantic.

Yet Doenitz did not give up. He operated in other areas that had little appeal for him. In the Mediterranean his boats were too easily seen submerged in the clear blue water. Some boats even went to the Far East. Surprisingly, his campaign in the Indian Ocean produced substantial results in the latter part of the war. From the spring of 1943 to the end of the war, more than a hundred ships were sunk in that area. In the long run, however, the sinkings counted for nothing. They had no influence on the trade lifelines or the British blockade.

The Far Eastern effort was a symbolic gesture of cooperation with the Japanese that was at least novel in approach. Some of the subs carried a gliding helicopter. Officially, a Focke-Achgelis FA300, it was popularly known as *Bachstelze*. The purpose of the plane was to add an extra range of vision for the commander.

The parts of the plane were carried in the boat. When the proper moment arrived, the plane was put together on the gun platform where it took off on rails. There was no motor, and it remained in the air by being pulled like a kite. If an emergency arose, the rotors could be jettisoned for a quicker descent. The novelty was intriguing, but German science would have to do better than that to win the war. Only the arrival of the new Type XXI boats could make a difference. The U-boat men patiently waited.

10

INVASION

As the new year 1944 began, Doenitz was sure that he had something up his sleeve that would alter the course of the war. It was not a new boat. Still, it was very important. There was little doubt that the Allies planned an invasion of the Continent soon, so his surprise arrived just in the nick of time.

One of the fundamentals of submarine operation that had plagued submariners of all nations was the need to surface to recharge batteries. For years men had hoped that a boat could be designed to remain underwater for long periods of time. Yet it seemed impossible. Now, Doenitz, after prodding his technicians, had the impossible development in the palm of his hands. He knew how his boats could stay submerged for days and days.

The answer to the German dreams was the *Schnorchel* (nose). That is exactly what it was, a nose to help the boat breathe. It let in air and let out gas so that the diesels could operate beneath the sea to recharge the batteries.

The periscope provided vision. The *schnorchel*, which also stuck out of the water when in use, provided life. It had two tubes that were so small above the water that no radar could pick them up on a screen. The longer tube was for air induction, the shorter tube for emitting gases from the engine. Hydraulic pressure raised the tubes to their operating position.

The Germans could not take credit for this invention, and it was strange that it had not been adopted by the U-boat arm long before. According to Samuel Eliot Morison, the American naval historian, Simon Lake, a pioneering submarine inventor in the United States, understood the principle as early as 1900. The first people who made the principle work were the Dutch.

At the start of the war, the Germans captured two Royal Netherlands Navy submarines that included such a device, but they ignored it for a long time. They were confident that they would make short work of the war and would not need the device. Late in 1942, with their hopes of a short war crushed, they took another look at the Dutch equipment and experimented with it. Even then there were delays, and no operational U-boats were fitted out with *schnorchels* before the early months of 1944.

The *schnorchel,* called "snorkel" by the Americans and "snort" by the British, was not a perfect instrument. The advantages were obvious. The more subtle drawbacks did not make them popular with U-boat commanders, however. Psychologically, submariners had the attitude and temperament necessary to remain underwater for long periods, so that did not bother them. They saw the big advantage of a refuge under the sea. It was the technical dangers that worried them.

When the long steel snorkel pipe was above the surface, there was always the chance that a wave could close the float valve and choke off the oxygen in the boat. The wind might also cause the exhaust gases to reenter the boat. The dangers of carbon monoxide poisoning and asphyxiation were real, and the engineers had to be prepared to switch to electric motors at the first sign of trouble. Even without asphyxiation, the variations in pressure could be harmful to the health of the crew. Finally, when the snorkel operated, the diesels made so much noise that the submarine sound gear was useless.

The many disadvantages of the snorkel were still outweighed by the advantages. Once again, U-boat men had to accept risk and go on with their jobs. Doenitz still looked forward to the completion of the new boats under construction to regain the initiative, but for now the addition of the snorkel to the old boats would have to do. This was a big step forward.

With the Allied invasion of the Continent imminent, boats with snorkels were the Germans' great hope of sinking cargo ships carrying supplies for the big landing.

The Germans made frantic preparations to forestall the anticipated invasion. In addition to the snorkel, they had a new acoustic torpedo that homed in on the sound of an enemy ship's propeller. Yet most of their basic calculations fell short. Hitler was certain that Norway would be a landing area, and Doenitz formed a group of ten boats, identified as *Mitte* to disrupt Allied advances there. Again, Hitler's intelligence was wrong. The next step was to form a group of boats in the Bay of Biscay to prevent an attack on that part of the French coast. They were called *Landwirt*. Some but not all of the boats were equipped with snorkels. Doenitz was sure that the boats without snorkels were doomed, but he did not hold them back.

On June 6, 1944, after months of careful planning, General Dwight D. Eisenhower gave the order for Operation Overlord to begin. Six hundred warships, four thousand amphibious craft and other small ships, and 176,000 men landed on the beaches of Normandy with hundreds of Allied planes overhead. It was the largest amphibious operation in history.

American intelligence was more accurate than Hitler's. Eisenhower and his staff knew of *Landwirt* and were ready for it on D day. Patrols of destroyers, jeep carriers, and shore-based planes protected the invasion forces from submarine attacks. Mine fields were also laid along the Brittany coast to blow up U-boats that sneaked along the shore.

In the early minutes of June 6, messages flashed to Doenitz that Allied paratroopers were landing in Normandy. He wasted no time in ordering his boats into action. Fifteen boats headed for the narrow, shallow English Channel, and fourteen boats patrolled the Bay of Biscay.

Air Chief Marshal Sir Sholto Douglas claimed that he had "a solid wall of air patrols" that would stop any undersea threats. Probably no one knows exactly what happened in the skirmishes offshore that wild day but the Coastal Command succeeded in forcing U-boats to return to their bases.

The next three days were worse for the U-boat commanders. In this hopeless situation, British planes sank five boats and damaged seven others. By the end of the month, eight more boats had gone down. Although some U-boat men found a few opportunities to attack, they were the exceptions. During June they sank two English frigates, a corvette, and an empty troopship, and they damaged four Liberty ships. Yet this meant practically nothing to the overwhelming invasion forces.

Despite their lack of success in hampering the invasion, the U-boats continued to enter the heavily guarded English Channel. They accomplished little except to lose twenty-five boats there and seven more in the Bay of Biscay. It was almost a suicide mission.

Worse was to come. As the Allied troops fought their way through France, the impregnable sub bases fell into their hands. Anticipating their seizure, Doenitz ordered the boats at Brest, Lorient, and Saint-Nazaire south to Bordeaux and La Pallice and then later to Norway.

In the cross-channel invasion the U-boats had failed. Many valuable crews, amounting to almost eight hundred men, had been lost. What would Doenitz do now?

Only extreme dedication to the fuehrer and his unworthy cause gave Doenitz the strength to fight a war that was almost certainly lost. Among the growing lists of dead and missing were two of his own sons. Yet he continued to send men to almost certain death. He even deceived himself and Hitler, whom he admired so much, by raising false hopes.

Doenitz could not control the casualty figures that he faced every day. Nonetheless, he continued to look for clouds with silver linings. The snorkel, the acoustic torpedo, and the new antiradar devices were important developments, yet the losses continued to climb. Now he placed his hope in the arrival of the Type XXI boats in the near future. Soon they would be off the ways.

Doenitz had always been popular with his men. He had taken trouble to become acquainted with them in the early days, and they followed him loyally. Now he was too busy to know many of the crews, and perhaps that was just as well. He could be sending many more to their death in the next few months.

Most of the aces had been killed. Lüth and Schnee were still alive, but they were among the few. The inexperienced commanders, however, took their boats out without hesitation. The tragedy for them was that they did not have time to gain experience. With the invasion completed, the only alternative left for the U-boats was to go out on the high seas again. The losing battle went on in the Atlantic.

11

THE CAPTURE OF U-505

Men at war were always curious about the enemy. Aside from seeing them as a source of valuable intelligence, they are intrigued by the men and machines they opppose. In the Atlantic, Allied sailors wondered about the strange U-boat men. What sort of people were they to spend so much of their lives underwater in such horrible conditions? Who were these men who were so eager to kill them? Why were they so mesmerized by Hitler? And now, with the odds so much against them, why did they continue to risk their lives?

U-boat survivors picked up by the Allies were always surrounded by their rescuers, who stared at them in amazement. The Allies took good care of the Germans despite the attacks these bedraggled men had made on their own lives just a short time before. The intrigue outweighed the enmity. The Allied sailors found that some of their foes were, as expected, arrogant and bitter; others were friendly and grateful. They differed as all humans do.

There was also a keen interest in the U-boat itself. To capture one was the goal of every American antisubmarine man. They could learn about the latest secret equipment, secret codes, and secret manuals. Then there was simply the adventurous aspect. What could be more dramatic than to board an enemy ship and conquer it? All the dramatic sea stories could be dwarfed by such an episode. The men of the *Spencer* had achieved half of the dream by boarding a boat. The other half, bringing a boat back to port, remained to be done.

The British had captured U-570 earlier in the war and converted it into H.M.S. *Graph*. Since then the war had changed. There was more scientific information to gather, and besides, Americans wanted to claim a boat of their own. So far, they had been unsuccessful.

Captain Daniel Gallery, commander of a hunter-killer group and captain of the baby aircraft carrier *Guadalcanal* was a vigorous, self-confident fighter who never minded attracting attention to himself. He called his ship "Can Do" and expected his men to live up to the name at all times.

In addition to the carrier, Gallery's group consisted of a screen made up of the destroyer *Forrest* and four smaller destroyer escorts. Gallery knew the value of intensive training, and he gave much attention to his aircraft operating at night. No U-boat would have a moment's peace around the clock if he could help it.

In April 1944 Kapitänleutnant Werner Henke, commander of U-515, ran across Gallery and his group escorting a convoy that had steamed out of Casablanca. In the early evening hours he became aware that he was being tracked by aircraft. He submerged until about midnight, when he thought it would be safe to surface, and was immediately attacked by two Avengers. Henke escaped, but a few hours later a fighter plane dropped depth charges on the boat, and the pursuit continued through the night.

About 1030 the next morning, the destroyer escort *Pope* received a sound contact close to the *Guadalcanal* and made a number of hedgehog and depth charge attacks. One

**Captain Daniel Gallery (left) with Lieutenant Albert David, who
headed the first party that went aboard to capture German U-505.**
(PHOTO: U.S. NAVY)

hit the U-515's pressure hull. For the next few hours, the escorts kept a careful vigil, and about 1,300 large oil bubbles from the damaged boat appeared on the surface.

Henke had dropped to 600 feet before he could gain control of the boat and attempt to rise. When he finally started up again, the destroyer escort *Chatelain* dropped depth charges. The U-515 broke the surface near the *Chatelain* and was clearly visible to the carrier crew. The *Chatelain* and another escort, the *Flaherty,* opened fire as an Avenger let go with rockets and two fighter planes strafed the boat.

Overwhelmed, Henke ordered his men to abandon the U-boat. The time was 1512, and the boat went down for the last time. Henke and forty-three of his men were picked up.

This was a successful score for Gallery, but it set him to thinking. With just a bit more luck he might have captured the boat. That would have been a feather in his cap that he would have enjoyed immensely. The hoped-for dream had almost become a reality.

In the next few weeks, the hunter-killer groups sank other submarines without any opportunity to capture a boat. They had certainly caught boats refueling in the mid-Atlantic. Their luck in jumping on U-boats during such operations caused Doenitz to order his boats to return to base before they ran out of fuel. The refueling procedure was too dangerous.

Although the U-boats were against the ropes, they still made plenty of trouble for the Allies. Time after time, they appeared where least expected. Often they showed up in areas they had not patrolled for months and found their enemy had become overconfident and complacent. That gave them their chance to strike.

At the end of May, U-549 sighted the CVE *Block Island* on its way to relieve another hunter-killer group in the vicinity of the Madeira and Cape Verde Islands. The boat torpedoed the carrier and then skillfully slipped inside the screen and let go with another torpedo. The carrier's rudder jammed, and the ship lost way when a third torpedo struck. The *Block Island* was finished. The U-549 had accomplished the rare feat of sinking an American carrier, the only one lost in the Atlantic. Still, U-549 was not finished.

The destroyer escort *Eugene Elmore* sighted the sub's periscope and went after it without result. Then U-549 spotted the destroyer escort *Barr*, sent an acoustic torpedo into its stern, and badly damaged the ship.

But U-549 did not give up the battle. While the crew of the *Block Island* abandoned ship, the submarine fired a torpedo at the *Elmore* and missed. While one escort rescued men from the carrier, the other escorts searched frantically for the U-boat. About 1,800 yards away the *Elmore* received a contact and attacked with hedgehogs. It was now 2120 in a very long, strenuous day. This time the *Elmore* had the last word. Heavy explosions below left no doubt that U-549 had finished its fighting days.

In the middle of May, Gallery and his group set out from Hampton Roads, Virginia, for the African coast. Since his experience with the U-515, Gallery had mulled over the possibility of capturing a U-boat and worked up a plan. He ordered each ship in his group to form and train a boarding party. It sounded like the days of the Barbary pirates or the War of 1812. It also sounded like a hopeless cause with one chance in a million. Nevertheless, the carefully selected men learned their job in the event the day ever arrived.

While invasion forces gathered for D day, Gallery sailed the Atlantic far from the center of action. After four quiet days of dismal searches, a disappointed Gallery ordered his ships to Casablanca for fueling. No sooner had he given the order than Lieutenant Commander Dudley Knox, captain of the *Chatelain*, reported a "possible sound contact."

Despite all of the scientific innovations, contacts were often fuzzy. A variety of noises or floating objects still threw off radar and sound operators. A "possible contact" was a long way from a sure thing.

At 1112 on June 4, however, the *Chatelain* contact was identified as a sub, and, with two other DEs, the ship started to attack. Above, fighters circled the area.

The bird's-eye view of the Wildcat pilots may have changed the course of battle. When the *Chatelain* started a second run, the airmen spotted the dark shape of the sub under the water. They shouted over the TBS (Talk between Ships), "You're going in the wrong direction, come back!" To nail down the exact location, the pilots fired machine gun rounds into the water. Knox later claimed that the pilots merely confirmed his decision. At any rate, they were working together, and the DE continued the attack.

The boat was the U-505, a Type IX. Larger than the more common Type VII, it was 252 feet long and displaced 1,100 tons. The normal crew consisted of four officers and fifty-six men. On the surface it could do a slightly speedier 19 knots and stay at sea for ninety days when cruising at an economical speed. The boat had four torpedo tubes forward, two tubes in the stern, and it carried a hefty load of twenty-one torpedoes. On deck antiaircraft guns replaced the 4.1-inch gun that had once been used.

The U-505 had survived a number of patrols and had a much longer career than many U-boats. Under three commanders it had also done more than its share of damage.

The present commander was Oberleutnant Harald Lange. He brought his boat up to periscope depth to see what was going on, saw more enemy action than he wanted, and dived. The sea was slightly rough, making it hard to keep the submarine at periscope depth. Yet he had seen enough to make his decision. He saw what he thought were three destroyers and far off an object that could be a carrier. He also had a glimpse of a plane but did not take a second look because he did not want to be seen. He assumed that there was a good chance that the pilot saw the large wake that his rolling boat made under the surface.

Diving deeper, Lange heard two bombs explode at a distance and, soon afterward, the sound of depth charges. The depth charges did the damage. Water broke into the boat, the electricity went off, and the rudder jammed.

The determined *Chatelain* had dropped twelve 600-pound depth charges that were set to go off at a shallow depth. The charges penetrated the outer hull, and the boat went over on its beam-ends. Inside the boat, the men and equipment tumbled about. Many of the crew were sure that the boat was sinking and rushed madly to the conning tower.

Lange may have lacked the experience to handle the desperate situation. Perhaps no one could have done any better under the circumstances. Once started, panic spreads like wildfire, and certainly Lange did not have much of a choice. He could go up or down. He went up.

Breaking the surface, Lange found the enemy ready for him. Three destroyer escorts opened fire, and fighter planes machine-gunned the boat. The time was 1122. Knox, with only the thought of sinking the boat on his mind, fired a torpedo, which missed.

Lange was the first on the bridge when the boat surfaced. The nearest ship shot shrapnel into the conning tower. Lange, hit in both knees and legs, fell down. Still conscious, he gave the order to abandon and scuttle the boat. The first officer, who had followed Lange to the bridge, had also been wounded and was lying on the starboard side with blood streaming down his face.

Soon, Lange lost consciousness for a spell. He did not know how long he was out, but when he revived he saw a number of men running around the deck trying to get life rafts clear. When one of the shells had exploded, Lange had been blown onto the main deck. He could not get up, and he tried to drag himself aft. Then he ended up in the water, not sure how he got there. He thought he was probably blown off by another explosion. His life jacket had been punctured, yet he remained afloat until two of his crew brought him a raft and pushed him into it. He could not see too well because he had been struck in the face and eye with splinters of wood, and his right eyelid was pierced with a splinter. Nevertheless, he saw some of his men on board the boat and ordered the men near him to give three cheers for the sinking boat.

The American version of the Nazi plight was not so heroic. As they saw it, the Germans were ready to give up. They streamed out of the conning tower with their hands above their heads while the boat circled at a speed of about four or five knots.

Gallery, following the action from the *Guadalcanal*, realized that the boat might be taken intact. With the fight apparently gone out of the Germans, the order was given for the Americans to cease fire. Then Gallery announced that he wanted the boat captured.

Shortly, "Away all boarding parties" was sounded, and a small band of men led by Lieutenant (j.g.) Albert David of the *Pillsbury* took off in a whaleboat. No one knew what to expect. If past experiences meant anything, Germans were down below preparing to scuttle the boat. Many U-boat commanders had done exactly that. It was a standard procedure. The ace, "Silent Otto" Kretschmer, was one example.

David was in a ticklish spot. All kinds of possibilities must have rushed through his head as he sailed forward in the little boat. Coming alongside the submarine, the whaleboat appeared about the size of a gnat.

Quickly, David and petty officers Arthur Knispel and Stanley Wdowiak, jumped on board the submarine. The three men, with David in the lead, went down the conning tower ladder. German seamen could have easily picked them off as they descended the ladder. David later said that he felt like Jonah being swallowed by the whale. Luck was with them. No Germans were on board. Searching the submarine, the boarding party found valuable code books in the radio room. They also gathered up charts and operating instructions sent from Doenitz. It was an intelligence windfall.

Although the Americans had escaped a hand-to-hand struggle with the submariners, there was still the ugly possibility that they could go down with the boat. One of the men in the party, Zenon Lukosius, heard running water. Looking to see where it came from, he discovered a leak from a bilge strainer. He found a lid that had been taken off lying on the deck, put it back where it belonged, and probably saved the boat from upending.

While the men hastily carried out their work inside the boat, the ocean swells started pouring down the hatch of the low-lying boat. David, hoping to avoid being swamped, ordered the hatch closed. None of them were submarine men, and the thought of being trapped below could not have made them too comfortable. Fortunately, they were busy, and their minds were occupied.

The boat had not been scuttled because the anxious Germans in their rush to get out had not set the firing devices. The Americans soon discovered this and were relieved to find that at least they would not blow up. Still, the boat was going down by the stern and settling deeper. How were they going to get their prize back to port?

After the initial conquest by David and his men, Gallery sent Commander Earl Trosino over to the U-505. Trosino lacked submarine experience, too, but he had spent most of his life at sea as an engineer aboard tankers. When Trosino reached the boat, which was still circling, he could not open the hatch. A partial vacuum held it tight, and nothing could open it.

The submarine circled in the midst of Germans in the water, and the Americans fished one man out so he could show them how to open the hatch. The trick was very simple. The startled German showed them a little valve. It let air into the pressure hull that equalized pressure inside and outside. After overcoming the problem, the German went overboard again.

Trosino helped David and his men set up some pumps to increase the buoyancy of the boat, and after a lot of sweat and hard work, the *Guadalcanal* took the U-505 in tow and headed for Bermuda. The U-boat made a strange sight as it was pulled along with a large American ensign proudly displayed from the conning tower.

While the frantic work on the submarine went on, forty survivors of the U-505 were picked up and sent to the *Guadalcanal*. Among them was Oberleutnant Lange. He had been rescued by an escort ship and transferred to the carrier where Gallery gave him the news that his boat had been captured.

Every moment that the boat was under tow was tense. The tow could break, the sea could work up, the boat could capsize. Any one of a dozen other dangers could destroy the glorious feat. They remembered that the British had lost U-110 under tow.

Admiral Royal Ingersoll sent a fleet tug, *Abnaki*, to help out. The tug, better equipped for the job, took over the tow on June 7. Then the seaplane tender *Humboldt* arrived with an American submarine officer who understood the mysteries of the U-boat. He was Commander C. G. Rucker. By the next day he had the boat completely surfaced and sailing on an even keel. Slowly, the tow made its way with greater confidence.

The major concern then became security. This was a top

The U.S.S. *Guadalcanal* and the captured German U-505. (PHOTO: U.S. NAVY)

secret affair. The most valuable possessions from the capture were the code books. If the Nazis learned that their boat had been taken, they could easily change the code. Captain Gallery, in no uncertain terms, told the men of his group that not one word was to leak out. Everyone recognized the importance of secrecy, and his order was obeyed implicitly.

Among the things found on the U-505 was a book of no value, but of considerable amusement. Someone came across the book in Lange's cabin. It was called *Roosevelt's Kampf,* and it contained extreme Nazi propaganda that claimed that the President of the United States had started the war and intended to conquer the world. The book was sent to the President, who must have been entertained by the wild accusations. He placed it in his library at Hyde Park.

The tamed U-505, once the terror of the seas, can now be seen at the Chicago Museum of Science and Industry where it rests peacefully.

12

END OF GLORY

The snorkel subs caught the Allies off balance. They were much harder to find, and the wary U-boats now had better radar-interception gear. Admiral of the Fleet Sir Andrew Cunningham admitted that the Allies did not know quite how to cope with them for the moment. The war did not return to the heyday of the wolf packs, but the snorkel helped the U-boats return to solitary operations that took the Allies by surprise. U-boats roamed over the Mediterranean Sea and the Arctic and Indian oceans and back to the North Atlantic.

The U-boat raids created tragic individual losses that in the long run were little more than stumbling blocks in the Allied march to victory. As Hitler met reverses on land and in the air, he placed more importance on the U-boat despite the futility of his position. Nonetheless, the U-boats still had a potential for wide-scale destruction.

In 1944 the U.S. Navy had good reason to fear that the Nazi subs could cause havoc along the East Coast of America. With the war effort in disarray, the Nazis tried another wild attempt to land agents in the United States. Their initial effort in 1942 had proven such a complete failure that they had not followed up with similar schemes. Now, they believed another reckless effort might be worth the risk.

In July 1944, the U-1229 left Trondheim, Norway, to land a spy in Maine. The try was senseless, especially since the boat unnecessarily steamed on the surface off the Grand Banks even though it was equipped with a snorkel. On August 20 Lieutenant (j.g.) A. X. Brokas sighted the boat and immediately attacked. He knocked five German gunners overboard and damaged the boat. The U-boat commander dived, but he did not have enough power underwater, and the boat surfaced. Five Avengers greeted the boat with rockets and bombs.

The U-1229 went down. Fortunately for the crew, there was enough time for them to abandon the boat. Forty-two survivors were picked up, and among them was the lonely spy. He was Oscar Mantel who had worked as a bartender in the Yorkville section of New York City. His venture was less well financed than his predecessors' since he only had $2,000 to do any imaginable harm.

This failure did not stop the bizarre Nazi schemes. Grasping at straws, they developed another rash escapade. In November the U-1230 set out with the same improbable idea: to land secret agents in the United States. The saboteurs were a German and an American traitor. The U-1230 sailed into Frenchman's Bay, Maine, and dropped off the men near Egg Rock. They reached shore in a rubber boat and landed at Hancock Point. An alert young boy saw the strangers coming ashore and told the police, who informed the FBI.

The German was Erich Gimpel, and the American was William Colepaugh. The misfit American, a native of Connecticut, had once attended the Massachusetts Institute of Technology. While living in Boston, he became acquainted with German sailors on an interned ship in the harbor. Their Nazi philosophy attracted Colepaugh, and he became increasingly anti-American.

Eventually, Colepaugh was expelled from M.I.T., and early in 1941 he wandered to Philadelphia where he was arrested on a draft-evasion charge. He escaped jail by being allowed to enter the U.S. Navy. His career in the navy was short because of his extreme political attitudes. After four months in the service he was discharged. Footloose again, he worked as a mess boy on a ship bound for Lisbon, a notorious spy center. While there he offered his services to the Nazis.

The FBI trailed the two men to New York City, where they were arrested and placed in a federal prison. These unskillful agents were better financed than Mantel if not any more successful. Each man had $30,000 to spend on sabotage.

The story the two secret agents told the FBI caused a certain amount of alarm because it was so plausible. They claimed that U-boats equipped with guided missiles planned to bombard the American coast. Certainly the German buzz bombs aimed at London were a real menace at the time. The same thing could happen to the coastal United States. Only time would tell if the tale was true or false.

The U-1230 lingered off the Maine coast for a few days and sank a Canadian merchant ship. Pursued by a heavy array of antisubmarine ships and aircraft, it still managed to escape.

The most significant contribution that the U-boats made at the end of 1944 was to report the weather in the Atlantic. Submarines had been used as weather stations many times, but this mission was critical.

Two boats, U-1053 and U-1232, started sending daily weather reports from the Atlantic to a meteorological center in Germany. This vital information for forecasting future weather conditions helped Hitler plan a last major gamble to end the war in triumph. The strategy was for Field Marshal von Rundstedt's forces to make a grand attack while Allied planes were grounded by foul weather. This was no wild scheme. Gaining advance weather information was a scientific, sensible effort that apparently worked.

Doenitz radioed the commanders of U-1053 and U-1232 that their weather reports "carried decision for establishing the start of our major offensive in the West, begun 16 December." This was the beginning of the famous Battle of the Bulge.

The Allies had assumed that Hitler was near total defeat when he surprised them by launching a powerful advance in the thinly defended Ardennes Forest in Belgium and Luxembourg. A huge tank force and heavily armed German troops broke through the Allied lines on a 45-mile front and came close to victory. The German thrust was crushed only after a month of vigorous fighting. Finally, the exhausted Germans retreated back to the Rhine. The Wehrmacht was on its last legs.

During this battle, U-boats helped by returning to the British Isles and the Western Approaches. Only the snorkel made this possible. The Allies suffered some severe losses that, looking back, seem unnecessary. Perhaps the Allies had become a little too confident and had let down their guard. In the Irish Sea alone, U-boats sank nine merchant ships sailing without escorts and the H.M.S. *Thane*, an escort carrier. In the English Channel, the Belgian ship *Leopoldville*, serving as a troopship, lost more than 800 men. Probably most of them could have been saved after the initial explosion if the crew had been properly trained to abandon ship. Nothing could be taken for granted even at this late date in the U-boat war.

The snorkel boats continued to cause trouble after the Battle of the Bulge. As Hitler's Third Reich showed signs of crumbling, the U-boats carried on, trying to give some hope to a lost cause. During March 1945 the U-boats sank more ships than at any time since July 1943. Yet, whatever the damage, the success was temporary. Sooner or later, antisubmarine forces wiped out most of the boats operating

German crewmen on the deck as their U-66 leaves on patrol. This boat was sunk on May 6, 1944. (PHOTO: U.S. NAVY)

around Great Britain. The Allies, briefly baffled, were too well organized now to be stopped permanently by the German submarines, even with their snorkels.

On the quiet Eastern Sea Frontier there was little expectation that U-boats would again harass the American coast. Americans were sure now that threats of submarine-launched guided missiles were idle talk. Yet, here too, U-boats showed up. The plan of the U-boat staff was to make surprise attacks to force the Allies to spread their antisubmarine forces thinly over wide areas. Such tactics, they thought, would give them a chance to return to less well defended British waters.

The Nazi plan did not work, and many U-boat crews lost their lives in hopeless attempts. In early 1945 four boats patrolled near the American coast. Among them were the U-866 and U-879, which were sunk before they could do any harm. Nevertheless, the other boats caused considerable distress among the Americans. The U-857 torpedoed the tanker *Atlantic States* in the Gulf of Maine. Off Cape Cod, however, the sub was caught and sunk.

One of the more experienced commanders, Kapitänleutnant Gunther Pfeffer of U-548, sank a freighter off the Virginia coast in mid-April. Four days later he torpedoed the tanker *Swiftscout* off the Delaware Capes. Pfeffer cleverly eluded a powerful antisubmarine force and in another few days sank a second tanker. Pfeffer's luck was too good to last. By the end of the month his boat had been discovered, chased, and sunk with all hands lost.

On April 12 President Roosevelt suddenly died at his cottage at Warm Springs, Georgia. Americans everywhere were stunned by the news, and fighting ships of the U.S. Navy all over the world held memorial services for the President who had had such affection for the navy. A few ships, however, simply observed a minute of silence in respect for the President, because they were heavily engaged.

At this time, off the Grand Banks, the U-1235 and

U-880 attempted to penetrate a defensive barrier of ships. Although the Allies sank them, they feared that other boats might show up in the next few days. The fear was heightened when the U-518 was sunk on April 21.

Three other U-boats were at large. The U-546 had been sighted, but not destroyed. On April 24 the *Frederick C. Davis*, part of the screen of a hunter-killer group, made contact, but a few minutes later a torpedo crashed into the port side of the ship. A number of officers and men were immediately killed, and others on the flying bridge were blown overboard. Fires erupted on the *Davis*, and the ship started to break in two.

About a hundred men abandoned ship. They found that the sea offered no comfort. It was rough, cold, and shark-infested. Then, two of the *Davis*'s depth charges exploded. Other ships in the screen rushed to aid the men, but many died in the water. When the count was made, only 66 had survived out of a crew of 192. With the war in Europe so close to an end, their deaths seemed doubly tragic.

The hunt for the sub went on for hours. In the group was the experienced *Pillsbury*, which located the missing U-546 again. Still, U-546 evaded detection by using a *Pillenwerfer* to deceive the Americans.

The *Flaherty* dropped hedgehogs and depth charges that jolted the submarine but did no real damage. The U-546 was almost in the clear when the *Flaherty* picked up another contact. Three ships joined in the attack and failed again.

The U-546 waited about 600 feet below the surface. It remained submerged for hours and hours but could not stay down forever. On the surface, destroyer escorts waited. After enduring ten hours of steady depth charging, the U-546 had to come up for air. The boat rose to 160 feet and took a brutal beating at that level. The bridge was hit, the pressure hull had a big hole, and the damaged batteries sent chlorine gas throughout the boat.

The U-boat commander surfaced, fully realizing that a concentration of ships waited. Still, he did not give up. He sighted the *Flaherty* and fired a torpedo. It missed. The *Flaherty* returned two torpedoes, and they missed. Then the *Pillsbury, Keith, Neunzer,* and *Varian* joined the battle, and there was no chance for the boat to get away. Finally, an order was given to cease fire when the submarine began to sink. It went straight up in the air and then down.

Once the submarine was out of the way, the DEs diligently searched for survivors. Miraculously, thirty-three men, including the commander, were saved. According to their rescuers, the Nazis were still hostile after their capture.

The two remaining U-boats in this group, U-858 and U-805, escaped destruction. Their wartime careers were almost over anyway. The war was rapidly drawing to a close.

On April 30, 1945, Hitler, defeated everywhere, committed suicide in his Berlin bunker. For all practical purposes the war was over. The Russians advancing from the east and the Americans and British moving from the west crushed the remnants of the supposedly invincible Wehrmacht.

The outcome of the war had been evident for months. Yet Doenitz sent his men to sea until the final day of surrender. Most of these men went to almost certain death. It would have been the better part of valor for Doenitz to decommission his boats and save the men's lives. Such a thought was impossible for him to comprehend. He had a distorted sense of loyalty, and he supported Hitler to the finish. Although never an ardent Nazi, he served the fuehrer just as persistently as did Himmler and Goebbels. Continually he supplied Hitler with optimistic news in the last months to assure him that the war would eventually turn in their favor. The appearance of the Type XXI was, of course, his greatest hope.

After months of construction delays, a Type XXI was

ready for battle in April. Doenitz gave command of this highly valued boat to the handsome Kapitänleutnant Adalbert Schnee, an ace who had recently served on Doenitz's staff.

The long-awaited boat, U-2511, lived up to the highest expectations. Under the sea, Schnee sped away from a corvette at an astounding 16 knots. The boat was sure to create havoc. Doenitz directed the boats to the Panama area to pluck some targets. There was only one trouble. The boat had been commissioned too late.

On the way, Schnee received a message on May 4, 1945, to return to base. The war was over. This was almost too much for a dedicated U-boat man to take. The disappointed Schnee wondered whether or not he should obey the order. All kinds of thoughts ran through his head. He knew that he had the potential for tremendous destruction at his fingertips. Why stop now when he knew that he could amaze the world with his new boat?

Schnee talked over the situation with his officers. One idea was to sail to Argentina, and another was to launch an attack. Reluctantly, after much talk, Schnee decided to return to base.

On the return voyage, Schnee sighted a heavy cruiser through his periscope. The target was perfect, and he could not resist an attack. Without any difficulty, he evaded the screen and went after the big ship. At the last moment, however, he came to his senses and let the opportunity pass.

The man who succeeded Hitler was none other than Doenitz. He had been named by the fuehrer in his final hours. Now, Doenitz became head of the Third Reich. As he saw it, he had only one duty: to end the war as quickly as possible. All hope was gone, and even he had become sickened with the useless deaths.

May 5 was the day of surrender for the U-boats. Contrary

to their orders, many commanders scuttled their boats rather than surrender.

Yet, even stranger, the U-boat war did not end on May 5. On that same day, U-853, a snorkel boat, patrolled off Narragansett Bay and came across the coal-carrying ship, *Black Point*. The U-boat torpedoed the ship, and unfortunately twelve men lost their lives.

Almost at once, antisubmarine ships in the area set out to sink the sub. At 2028 the destroyer escort *Atherton* picked up a sound contact only five miles from Block Island. Immediately, the warship dropped depth charges and hedgehogs. The water was a mere 15 fathoms deep, and yet the U-853 sat on the bottom and escaped damage.

The *Atherton* lost sound contact with the submarine for about three hours and then picked it up again. This time, the *Atherton's* hedgehog attack destroyed U-853 with the entire crew. They certainly died in vain.

The antisubmarine force was not absolutely certain that the U-853 was sunk, and they continued their attack through the morning of May 6. Finally enough of the submarine remains came to the surface to convince the Americans that the U-boat was finished. Part of the evidence was the sub commander's cap.

On May 7 the Germans and Americans signed an agreement of unconditional surrender by the Germans, and the next day the Russians also signed. May 8, 1945, became the official V-E (victory in Europe) Day.

With the war over in Europe, the U-boats received orders to surface, lower the Kriegsmarine ensign, fly a black flag, and go to a designated port. The dejected crews laid oil-soaked ensigns on the decks and burned them. The once-proud U-boats, undersea terrors, became a thing of the past. The antisubmarine forces, once the underdog, had prevailed.

Few boats were in the western Atlantic at the time of

German crew members from a captured U-boat come ashore at Norfolk, Virginia. (PHOTO: U.S. NAVY)

surrender, but Kapitänleutnant Bernardelli in U-805, gave up off Cape Race, Newfoundland, and was taken to the Portsmouth Navy Yard at Kittery, Maine.

Off the Delaware Capes, the U-858 did not have a black flag so it flew two old blankets. A few others also gave up along the coast. One cargo submarine, U-234, on its way to Tokyo via the Atlantic, surrendered to the destroyer escort *Sutton* and joined U-805, U-873, and U-1228 at the Portsmouth Navy Yard. The U-234's situation was a little different. It carried two Japanese officers who insisted on committing suicide before the surrender.

The German crews must have had mixed thoughts at the time. Whether they knew it or not, they were lucky to be alive. Germans estimated that 32,000 of a total of 39,000 U-boat men had died in the war. According to the British Admiralty Assessment Committee, which worked on an appraisal with the U.S. Navy Tenth Fleet, 1,179 U-boats had been used in the war. Of that number, 699 were sunk by the Allies and 82 were lost in accidents or destroyed by unknown causes.

Despite the opportunity to put the war behind them, two U-boat commanders refused to give up. Their boats were U-530 and U-977. The U-530, off Long Island, made a number of attacks on convoys after the surrender. Luckily for the Allies, the attacks failed. Then the commander headed for Argentina where he thought he would receive a warm welcome. On July 9, more than two months after V-E Day, U-530 arrived at Mar del Plata on the Argentine coast, where the crew was quickly interned.

Heinz Schaeffer of the second boat, U-977, was an experienced submariner but a new commander. At the age of twenty-four he took over the command of U-977 on Christmas 1944. Late in April 1945 the boat arrived at Christiansund South, a Norwegian base. While there, Schaeffer learned on the radio that the Germans had no intention of surrendering. The news broadcast falsely claimed that Hitler had been killed in the "Battle of Berlin" and correctly stated that Doenitz was now in charge of the government. The expectation was that the war would be carried on from Norway.

On May 2 Schaeffer left the base on another war cruise with the words of his flotilla commander ringing in his ears: "Fight on to the very end. Germany will never, never surrender." Carefully, Schaeffer headed for the coast of England. At the time, the British estimated that the life expectancy of a U-boat crew was forty days. Schaeffer was inclined to agree with them.

While at sea, the commander received the surrender message and instructions that he was to take orders from the Allied command on the next day. Schaeffer, like many of his fellow commanders, was shocked by the announcement. The whole idea that Doenitz, as head of state, would give up was inconceivable. The firm belief in no surrender persisted. Schaeffer thought at first that the message was an Allied trick.

The more Schaeffer mulled over the surrender order, true or false, the more he was determined not to abide by it. The next day, he admitted to himself that the order must be correct even though he doubted that Doenitz had formally surrendered. He talked about the situation with his crew and pictured the devastation of a Germany under the Allies. He also raised hopes of a better life in Argentina. Both Schaeffer and one of the engineers knew the South American country where they had friends and believed that many of the people held views similar to the Nazi philosophy. It might well be their land of opportunity.

After laying the groundwork, the commander sprang his idea to sail for Argentina. The men were to make their decision by a democratic vote. Thirty of the forty-eight were ready to follow their leader to South America. Two wanted to go to Spain, which certainly seemed more practical. Spain was closer and was a fascist nation under General Francisco Franco. Oddly, this idea was not well received. Sixteen dissenters, most of them married petty officers, simply wanted to go home to their families.

Schaeffer said that he wanted only men who shared his views for the long and dangerous voyage. So he sailed into Norwegian waters near Bergen on the night of May 10, surfaced, and sent the sixteen men on their way in rubber boats.

According to Schaeffer, the long journey to Argentina began with a unified group. Caution was the key word. The Allies were still the enemy. They had no wish to attack them, but they had every wish to avoid capture. The ocean was still patrolled by the Allies, and evasion was not easy.

Schaeffer planned to remain underwater, using the U-997's snorkel, as long as possible. Only men steeped in the fanaticism of Naziism dared dream of such a venture. Their high hopes were fueled with the thought of a friendly welcome when they arrived at their destination.

At the start, spirits were high, but as the days dragged on the tension increased. The stifling atmosphere in the boat affected the men physically and mentally. They needed sunlight and exercise on deck. Even more, they needed to get rid of the garbage that bred flies and maggots. Yet there was no way to dump the mess without the possibility of detection while they were submerged.

Diversions such as card games held little attraction after a while. Men stood watch, ate, slept. Day or night, they followed the same dull routine. Locked in their underwater prison they had no escape. They had committed themselves.

After two or three weeks on their slow way, mechanical troubles erupted. The diesels were on the verge of breaking down, but somehow the crew managed to make repairs, and they plodded onward. Whenever the snorkel went up, the men feared that they were being picked up by enemy radar. At times, they were sure that depth charges would drop on them in the next few minutes.

By the end of seven long weeks under the sea, most of the men were close to cracking up. The filth grew worse. Schaeffer realized that they must get rid of the refuse. He decided that they must unload a torpedo and force the garbage out of the tube with compressed air. That was a tough job for weakened men. The senior watch officer let Schaeffer know in no uncertain terms that it would be easier to fire a torpedo than to unload it. There was no question that was true. Also, if they fired all the torpedoes, they would gain some valuable space. The strong-minded Schaeffer disagreed. He knew that he had to retain a firm grasp on his command, too. He wanted to keep all the torpedoes, he claimed, to prove that none had been fired after the surrender, and he made his order stick.

In the heat of the summer, the food became moldy, the bulkheads turned green in the humid air, and the unwashed men developed rashes and boils. The pallid, bearded men looked like ghosts as they listlessly went about their duties. Although bickering among them increased, surprisingly they were not at one another's throats. Perhaps they were too weak to conspire.

One injured man developed a seriously infected arm. Schaeffer took it upon himself to be the doctor. Something had to be done at once before the man died. He gave the sailor a bottle of beer as an anesthetic, froze the arm, and then pierced it to let out the poisonous pus. With some care, the man improved. Schaeffer considered it a near thing. He had made up his mind to put into port or transfer the patient to a passenger ship to save his life. That would mean the end of their dream.

After weeks of worsening conditions, the crew's grumbling mounted, and even Schaeffer wondered to himself if it was all a mistake. It was incredible that they had survived this long. Outwardly, the commander remained the stern disciplinarian. He knew that all would be lost if he could not keep firm control.

Forty, fifty, sixty days under the sea and the boat was still on course for Argentina. Schaeffer looked at his men, and they appeared to him like corpses. Condensation dripped down from the bulkheads continually, and everything in the boat was wet. When not on duty, the men went to their bunks in a stupor.

After sixty-six days, an endurance record never before achieved, Schaeffer ordered the boat to surface at night. They rose slowly. As the great moment arrived, Schaeffer later wrote, "Elation swept over me, a sense that life had begun again for all of us. The compressed air came hissing into our tanks, the depth gauge in the conning tower started moving—why it was racing! It was like going up in a lift."

There were no ships in sight, and as soon as possible most of the crew came up on deck. The poor radio operator and engineers remained below, but even they had the pleasure of knowing that fresh air rushed through the hatch.

When daylight arrived, the boat submerged again. Life was different now. Spirits skyrocketed. The drawn, weak men found new hope. Soon their ghastly journey would be over.

Schaeffer later wrote about the voyage and may have distorted some of the story, but his conclusion has a ring of truth. He claimed that the lesson he learned was that the energy and willpower of one person could make the difference to the fate of everyone on board. No one could argue that Schaeffer lacked willpower.

The U-977 still had a long way to go before reaching Argentina. Much of the time they were on the surface and made better distances. Now no one wanted to sleep or eat below, and the men spent much of the time on deck.

Hammocks were strung between the guns, and sometimes they fished for sport and a change in their miserable menu.

On August 17, 1945, they accomplished the impossible by arriving at Mar del Plata. At the three-mile limit, the crew flashed a signal in English that this was a German submarine, and then the men stopped the engines. An Argentine naval officer came on board and permitted Schaeffer to take the boat into the harbor.

The greeting that the crew of the U-977 received was not exactly what they had envisioned. They were immediately interned and placed on an Argentine cruiser. Soon they were transferred to the jurisdiction of the U.S. government and served many months in prison. The U-977 was eventually destroyed. The war was over for the officers and men, the last Nazi holdouts.

The U-boats had caused terrible damage during the six years of war. They had sunk about 3,000 ships amounting to millions and millions of tons. The tragic Allied loss at sea of about 40,000 persons during this period is small only when compared with the casualties for one day at Hiroshima.

Despite the horrifying statistics, the U-boats had failed. They did not succeed in blockading Great Britain, stopping the flow of American military men and supplies to the European theater of war, or gaining control of the seas.

The convoy system, the scientific achievements, and the courage of the men of the Allied navies and merchant marine conquered the undersea terror that had threatened not only the freedom of the seas but also the freedom of the world.

Under the guise of professionalism, Doenitz and his men served Hitler well. The world would have been much better off if they had looked beyond their technical ability, thoughtless loyalty, and professional pride to question the leadership of the Third Reich. Many individual actions of

U-boat commanders showed remnants of their humane feelings, but when all was said and done, they merely aided and abetted a cruel cause. Their daring, endurance, and fortitude did not serve civilization well.

BIBLIOGRAPHY

Books

Busch, Harald. *U-Boats at War.* New York: Ballantine, 1955.
Cope, Harley F. *Serpent of the Seas.* New York: Funk & Wagnalls, 1942.
Doenitz, Karl. *Memoirs—Ten Years and Twenty Days.* Cleveland: World, 1959.
*Frank, Wolfgang. *The Sea Wolves.* New York: Ballantine, 1981.
Gallery, Daniel. *Twenty Million Tons under the Sea.* Chicago: Henry Regnery, 1956.
*Hoyt, Edwin. *U-Boats Offshore.* New York: Stein & Day, 1978.
*Hughes, Terry, and John Costello. *The Battle of the Atlantic.* New York: Dial, 1976.
*Mac Intyre, Donald. *U-Boat Killer.* New York: Bantam, 1979.
Martiensen, Anthony. *Hitler and His Admirals.* New York: Dutton, 1949.
Morison, Samuel E. *History of United States Naval Operations in World War II*, Vols. I, IX. Boston: Little, Brown, 1947, 1956.
Rush, C. W., W. C. Chambliss, and H. J. Gimpel. *The Complete Book of Submarines.* Cleveland: World, 1958.
*Schaeffer, Heinz. *U-Boat 977.* New York: Bantam, 1981.
*Showell, J. P. Mallman. *U-Boats under the Swastika.* New York: Arco, 1974.
Smith, S. E., ed. *The United States Navy in World War II.* New York: Morrow, 1966.
*Stafford, Edward P. *The Far and the Deep.* London: Barker, 1968.

Von der Porten, Edward. *The German Navy in World War II.* New York: Crowell, 1969.

*Waters, John M., Jr. *Bloody Winter.* Princeton, N.J.: Van Nostrand, 1967.

*Whitehouse, Arch. *Subs and Submariners.* Garden City, N.Y.: Doubleday, 1961.

Widder, Arthur. *Action in Submarines.* New York: Harper & Row, 1967.

Article

Whipple, A. B. C. "The Education of Willie." *Life,* Jan. 22, 1945.

*Easiest to read.

About the Author

Ernest A. McKay teaches American and aviation history at the State University of New York–Maritime College. He is a graduate of Colgate University with a Ph.D. in history from New York University. During World War II, he served with the Third Amphibious Force in the Pacific and participated in landings at Leyte and Lingayen Gulf, and the battle for Leyte Gulf. During the Korean conflict he was a Lieutenant Commander, USNR, on the staff of the Under Secretary of the Navy. He is the author of numerous articles and four other books; the most recent, *A World to Conquer*, was selected as one of the best sci-tech books of 1981 by the *Library Journal*. Mr. McKay's previous book for young people is *Carrier Strike Force: Pacific Air Combat in World War II*.